5000 GERMAN WORDS

**Essential Vocabulary
for Examinations**

COLLINS
GEM

5000 GERMAN WORDS

compiled by

Barbara I. Christie MA (Hons)

and

Màiri MacGinn MA (Hons)

Collins
London and Glasgow

General Editor
Richard H. Thomas

First Published 1979
Reprinted 1986
ISBN 0 00 459301 4

© **William Collins Sons & Co. Ltd. 1979**

Printed in Great Britain by
Collins Clear-Type Press

HOW TO USE THIS BOOK

This book provides the user with a comprehensive range of vocabulary covering areas which are frequently the subject of language courses and exam questions, as well as wider interest areas which he may wish to discover for himself. There are 50 themes, each beginning with a basic list of nouns and building up the whole subject picture through appropriate verbs, example phrases, idioms etc. The lists are equally suited to memorization, perhaps as a class exercise, and for use in essays or letters, or in conversation groups.

The nouns themselves are divided into masculine, feminine and neuter genders. As a general rule, three different levels of difficulty have been given for each theme, marked with 1, 2 and 3 stars. These serve to split the vocabulary into manageable sections for easier learning. The 50 themes are further supplemented by separate vocabulary lists, grouped according to parts of speech, containing items which are not restricted to one theme or even to a few. This brings the total number of vocabulary items to 5000.

The user will find it easy to follow ideas from one theme to another: for instance, when he is describing his house he can progress from the general vocabulary under HAUS to more detailed vocabulary under HAUSHALT and MÖBEL. Similarly KÖRPERTEILE contains vocabulary for the basic parts of the body, while diseases and other afflictions can be found in GESUNDHEIT. The user will quickly become familiar with the layout of the German themes, which are arranged alphabetically, and an English version of the contents list is also provided on pages 10 and 11.

All plurals have been included in the text with the exception of feminine nouns ending in -in which are all regularly -innen in the plural, and those forms (in any gender) which remain the same for singular and plural.

Nouns formed from adjectives: masculine nouns are shown as follows

Tote(r), -n   dead man

indicating that the optional r is used with the indefinite article

but   **ein Toter**
       der Tote

Corresponding plurals are **Tote** and **die Toten**.

German words which have more than one meaning are marked by an asterisk (*) and a full list of such homonyms is given on page 235 with references to the various translations in different themes.

The final section in the book is a 'reminder' index allowing the user to find the German for words in the first two levels. This will serve as a valuable revision aid.

Abbreviations used in this book:

m	masculine
f	feminine
nt	neuter
pl	plural
n	noun
adj	adjective
adv	adverb
prep	preposition
conj	conjunction
acc	accusative
dat	dative
gen	genitive

8

INHALT *(Forts)*   **SEITE**

CONTENTS   PAGE

CONTENTS *(cont)*   PAGE

---

* MIT DEM AUTO UNTERWEGS *(m)*

der Autofahrer	motorist
der Fahrer	driver
der Führerschein, -e	driving licence
der Fußgänger	pedestrian
der Fußgängerüberweg	pedestrian crossing
der Gang*, ⸚e	gear
der Kilometer	kilometre
der Lastwagen	lorry
der Motor, -en	engine
der Motorschaden, ⸚	breakdown
der Parkplatz, ⸚e	parking space; car park; lay-by (*in country*)
der Polizist, -en	policeman
der Reifen	tyre
der Reifenschaden, ⸚	puncture; faulty tyre
der Scheibenwischer	windscreen wiper
der Scheinwerfer	headlight, headlamp
der Umweg, -e	detour
der Verkehr	traffic
der Verkehrsunfall, ⸚e	road accident
der Wagen*	car
der Weg*, -e	road, way
der Wohnwagen	caravan

* MIT DEM AUTO UNTERWEGS *(nt)*

das Auto, -s	car
das Benzin	petrol
das Gaspedal	accelerator
das Öl	oil
das Parkhaus, (-häuser)	(covered) car park
das Pedal, -e	pedal
das Rad*, ⸚er	wheel

fahren to go, drive
ein Auto fahren to (be able to) drive a car
mit dem Auto die Straße entlang fahren to drive along the street
stoppen, anhalten to stop

* MIT DEM AUTO UNTERWEGS (f)

die Autobahn, -en	motorway
die Autofahrerin	motorist
die Auto- Straßenkarte, -n	road map
die Bereifung (sg)	tyres
die Biegung, -en	bend, turn
die Bremse, -n	brake
die Fahrerin	driver
die Fahrt*, -en	journey, trip
die Garage, -n	garage
die Geschwindigkeit, -en	speed
die Hupe, -n	horn, hooter
die Kreuzung, -en	crossroads
die Kurve, -n	bend, corner
die Panne, -n	breakdown
die Polizistin	policewoman
die Reise, -n	journey
die (Reparatur)werkstatt, ⁻en	garage (for repairs), service station
die Straße, -n	road, street
die Straßenkarte, -n	road map, plan
die Straßenverkehrs- ordnung	Highway Code
die Tankstelle, -n	service station, garage
die Verkehrsampel (sg)	traffic lights
die Windschutz- scheibe, -n	windscreen

bremsen to brake; schalten to change gear
hupen to sound or toot one's horn
parken to park; to park the car
eine Fahrt machen to go for a drive
eine Fahrt von 3 Stunden a 3-hour journey
eine Reise von 3 Tagen a 3-day journey
gute Fahrt!, gute Reise! have a good trip!, have a
  good journey!
200 Kilometer in der Stunde machen, mit 200
  Stundenkilometern fahren to do 200 kilometres an
  hour

** MIT DEM AUTO UNTERWEGS (m)

der Abschleppwagen	breakdown van
der Anhalter	hitch-hiker
der Anlasser	starter
der Chauffeur, -s	chauffeur
der Fahrlehrer	driving instructor
der Fahrschüler	learner driver
der Geschwindigkeits-	
messer	speedometer
der Kilometerfresser	roadhog
der Kofferraum,	
(-räume)	boot
der Mechaniker	mechanic
der Motorradfahrer	motorcyclist
der Sicherheitsgurt, -e	seat belt
der Starter	starter
der Strafzettel	(parking) fine, ticket
der Tachometer	speedometer
der Tod	death
Tote(r), -n	dead man
der Tramper	hitch-hiker
der Verkehrsrowdy, -s	
or (-rowdies)	road hog
Verletzte(r), -n	casualty
der Wegweiser	sign, signpost

sich auf den Weg machen to set off
unterwegs on the way
gehen wir!, auf geht's! let's go!, off we go!
sich anschnallen to put on one's seat belt
den Motor anschalten/abschalten to switch on/
switch off the engine
der Motor or der Wagen springt nicht an the car
won't start
mein Auto ist kaputt my car has had it
den ersten Gang einlegen to engage first gear
beschleunigen, Gas geben to accelerate, to step on it
der Wagen fährt weg the car moves off
langsamer fahren to slow down; to drive more
slowly

** MIT DEM AUTO UNTERWEGS (f)

die Fahrlehrerin	driving instructress
die Fahrprüfung, -en	driving test
die Fahrschule, -n	driving school
die Fahrschülerin	learner driver
die Fahrstunde, -n	driving lesson
die Gasse, -n	alley, lane, back street
die geschlossene Ortschaft	built-up area
die Hauptverkehrsstraße	main road
die Hauptverkehrszeit	rush hour
die Marke, -n	make (of car)
die (Motor)haube, -n	bonnet
die Parkuhr, -en	parking meter
die Reifenpanne, -n	puncture
die (Reise)route, -n	route, itinerary
die Starterklappe, -n	choke
die Stoßstange, -n	bumper
die Straßenkreuzung	crossroads
die Tote, -n	dead woman
die Umleitung, -en	diversion
die Wegkreuzung, -en	crossroads

** MIT DEM AUTO UNTERWEGS (nt)

das Hinterrad, ⸚er	rear wheel
das Lenkrad, ⸚er	steering wheel
das Parkhochhaus, (-häuser)	multi-storey car park
das Rücklicht, -er	rear light
das Steuerrad, ⸚er	steering wheel
das Straßenschild, -er	road sign
das Trampen	hitch-hiking
das Verdeck, -e	hood
das Vorderrad, ⸚er	front wheel

die Ampel überfahren, bei Rot über die Kreuzung
fahren to go through the lights at red
die Windschutzscheibe splitterte the windscreen
shattered

*** MIT DEM AUTO UNTERWEGS (m)

der Anhänger*	trailer
der Blinker	indicator
der Caravan, -s	caravan
der Kreisverkehr, -e	roundabout
der Leerlauf	neutral (gear)
der Mietwagen	hired car
der Mittelstreifen	central reservation
der Rastplatz, "e	lay-by (large; in country)
der Richtungsanzeiger	indicator
der Rück(blick)spiegel	rear-view mirror
der Schupo, -s	'bobby'
der Sportwagen	sports car
der Vergaser	carburettor
der Verkehrspolizist, -en	traffic warden
der Wagenheber	jack

*** MIT DEM AUTO UNTERWEGS (nt)

das Armaturenbrett	dashboard
das Bankett, -e	hard shoulder (on motorway)
das Ersatzrad, "er	spare wheel
das Firmenauto, -s	company car
das Getriebe(gehäuse)	gearbox
das Nummernschild, -er	number plate
das Todesopfer	fatality

einen Platten haben to have a flat tyre
eine (Motor)panne haben to have a breakdown
mein Wagen ist stehengeblieben my car wouldn't go
etwas funktioniert nicht something is not working (right), there is something wrong
nach dem Motor schauen to have a look at the engine
mir ist das Benzin ausgegangen I've run out of petrol
vollmachen bitte! fill her up please!
das Auto reparieren lassen to have the car repaired

*** MIT DEM AUTO UNTERWEGS (f)

die Autoschlange, -n	line of cars
die Autowäsche, -n	car wash (*wash*)
die Karosserie	bodywork
die Klapperkiste, -n	banger, old car
die Kupplung, -en	clutch
die Limousine, -n	saloon car
die Notbremsung, -en	emergency stop
die Politesse, -n	(female) traffic warden
die Querstraße, -n	turning, junction
die Radkappe, -n	hubcap
die Raststätte, -n	service area
die Ringstraße, -n	ring road
die Verkehrspolizistin	traffic warden
die Verkehrsverletzung, -en	traffic offence
die Waschstraße, -n	car wash (*place*)
die (Weg)abzweigung, -en	turning, fork (in the road)
die Wendung, -en	U-turn
die Windungen (*pl***)**	twists and turns

überholen to overtake; **abbiegen** to turn off
mit quietschenden Reifen with a screech of brakes
sich verirren to get lost, take the wrong road
sich zurechtfinden to find one's way
per Anhalter fahren, trampen to hitch-hike
die Geschwindigkeit überschreiten to exceed the speed limit
mit voller Geschwindigkeit, mit Höchstgeschwindigkeit at full speed
er bekam einen Strafzettel für zu schnelles Fahren he was booked for speeding
schleudern to skid; **zusammenfahren** to run over
in ein Auto fahren to bump into a car
auf ein Auto auffahren to bump into a car (*from behind*)
der Wagen krachte gegen die Mauer the car crashed into the wall

* AUF DEM BAUERNHOF (m)

der Acker, ∷	field
der Bach, ∺e	stream, brook
der Bauer, -n	farmer; peasant, countryman
der Bauernhof, ∺e	farm, farmyard
der Boden*, ∺	ground; soil; floor; loft
der Hahn, ∺e	cock, rooster
der Hirte, -n	shepherd
der Hügel	hill
der Hund, -e	dog
der Karren	cart
der Landarbeiter	farm labourer
der Landwirt, -e	farmer
der Lieferwagen	van
der Ochse, -n	ox
der Pflug, ∺e	plough
der Schlamm	mud
der Traktor, -en	tractor
der Wald, ∺er	wood, forest

** AUF DEM BAUERNHOF (m)

der Bulle, -n	bull
der Esel	donkey
der Graben, ∺	ditch
der Hafer (sg)	oats
der Hase, -n	hare
der Haufen	heap, pile
der Heuboden, ∺	hayloft
der Heuhaufen	haystack
der Schäfer	shepherd
der Schäferhund, -e	sheepdog
der Stapel	pile
der Stier, -e	bull
der Teich, -e	pond
der Weizen	wheat
der Zaun, Zäune	fence

auf dem Bauernhof arbeiten to work on the farm
landwirtschaftlich agricultural

* AUF DEM BAUERNHOF (f)

die Bäuerin	lady farmer; farmer's wife; peasant woman
die Ente, -n	duck
die Erde	ground; soil, earth
die Ernte, -n	harvest; crop
die Gans, ¨e	goose
die Henne, -n	hen
die Katze, -n	cat
die Kuh, ¨e	cow
die Landschaft, -en	countryside, landscape
die Leiter, -n	ladder
die (Wind)mühle, -n	windmill
die Ziege, -n	goat

* AUF DEM BAUERNHOF (nt)

das Bauernhaus, (-häuser)	farmhouse
das Dorf, ¨er	village
das Feld, -er	field
das Huhn, ¨er	chicken, hen; (pl) poultry
das Kalb, ¨er	calf
das Küken	chicken, chick
das Land*, ¨er	land, country
das Pferd, -e	horse
das Schaf, -e	sheep
das Schwein, -e	pig
das Stroh	straw
das Tier, -e	animal

** AUF DEM BAUERNHOF (f)

die Erntezeit, -en	harvest (time)
die Heide, -n	heath

das Feld pflügen to plough the fields
im Feld arbeiten to work in the fields
der Schäfer paßt auf die Schafe auf the shepherd looks after the sheep

---

** AUF DEM BAUERNHOF (nt)

das Getreide	cereals, grain
das Heu	hay
das Korn, ̈er	corn, grain of corn
das Zugpferd, -e	carthorse

*** AUF DEM BAUERNHOF (m)

der Brunnen	well
der Dünger	dung; manure, fertilizer
der Eimer	bucket, pail
der Gutshof, ̈e	(big) farm
der Hühnerstall, ̈e	henhouse
der Kipper	tipper, dumper
der Kuhstall, ̈e	cow-shed, byre
der Mähdrescher	combine harvester
der Mais	maize
der Pferdestall, ̈e	stable
der Puter	turkey(-cock)
der Roggen	rye
der Schuppen	shed
der Schweinestall, ̈e	pigsty
der Stall, ̈e	stable; sty
der Truthahn, ̈e	turkey(-cock)

der Bauer sät das Getreide the farmer sows the seed
Weizen/Gerste anbauen to grow wheat/barley

*** AUF DEM BAUERNHOF (*f*)

die **Feldmaus,** (**-mäuse**)	fieldmouse
die **Furche, -n**	furrow
die **Gabel, -n**	pitchfork
die **Garbe, -n**	sheaf
die **Gerste**	barley
die **Herde, -n**	herd; flock
die **Kleie**	bran
die **Maul- und Klauenseuche**	foot-and-mouth disease
die **Milchkanne, -n**	milk churn
die **Pute, -n**	turkey
die **Scheune, -n**	barn
die **Truthenne, -n**	turkey
die **Vogelscheuche, -n**	scarecrow
die **Weide*, -n**	meadow; pasture
die **Wiese, -n**	meadow

*** AUF DEM BAUERNHOF (*nt*)

das **(Bauern)gut, ¨-er**	farm, farmstead
das **Federvieh**	poultry
das **Gatter**	gate (*of field*)
das **Geflügel**	poultry
das **Geschirr*, -e**	harness
das **Hühnerhaus,** (**-häuser**)	henhouse
das **(Rind)vieh**	cattle
das **Vieh**	livestock

die Hühner scharren in der Erde the hens scratch about in the earth

die Ernte einbringen *or* **einfahren** to bring in the harvest *or* the crops

zur Erntezeit, in der Erntezeit at harvest time

die Kühe weiden auf der Wiese the cows graze in the meadows

die Kühe sind auf der Weide the cows are out to graze

* BÄUME (m)

der Ast, ¨e	branch
der Baum, Bäume	tree
der Busch, ¨e	bush
der Christbaum	Christmas tree
der Eichbaum	oak
der Stamm, ¨e	trunk
der Tannenbaum	fir tree
der Wald, ¨er	wood, forest
der Weihnachtsbaum	Christmas tree
der Zweig, -e	branch

** BÄUME (m)

der Forst, -e	forest
der Kastanienbaum	chestnut tree
der Lindenbaum	lime tree
der Obstbaum	fruit tree
der Wipfel	tree-top

*** BÄUME (m)

der Ahorn, -e	maple
der Buchsbaum	box tree
der Mistelzweig, -e	(sprig of) mistletoe
der Strauch, Sträucher	bush
der Tannenzapfen	pine cone
der Weidenbaum	willow
der Weißdorn, -e	hawthorn
der Weinberg, -e	vineyard

auf einen Baum steigen *or* klettern to climb a tree
vom Baum fallen to fall off a tree
einen Baum fällen to fell a tree
der Stammbaum the family tree
ein Holzstuhl (m) a wooden chair
Weihnachtsdekorationen (*fpl*) Christmas decorations
Christbaumschmuck (*sg*) Christmas tree decorations
ein dünner Zweig a twig
ein Baumhaus a tree house

* BÄUME (*f*)

die Beere, -n	berry
die Birke, -n	birch
die Buche, -n	beech
die Eiche, -n	oak
die Linde, -n	lime tree
die Weide*. -n	willow

** BÄUME (*f*)

die Kastanie, -n	chestnut
die Knospe, -n	bud
die Rinde, -n	bark
die Ulme, -n	elm
die Wurzel, -n	root

*** BÄUME (*f*)

die Blutbuche, -n	copper beech
die Eibe, -n	yew
die Esche, -n	ash
die Fichte, -n	fir tree
die Föhre, -n,	
die Kiefer, -n	pine
die Pappel, -n	poplar
die Pinie, -n	pine
die Platane, -n	plane tree
die Roßkastanie, -n	horse chestnut
die Stechpalme, -n	holly
die Tanne, -n	fir tree
die Trauerweide, -n	weeping willow

*, **, *** BÄUME (*nt*)

das Blatt, ⸚er	leaf
das Geäst (*sg*)	branches
das Gebüsch (*sg*)	bushes
das Holz (*sg*)	wood (*substance*)
das Laub(werk) (*sg*)	leaves, foliage

im Herbst werden die Blätter gelb the leaves turn yellow in autumn

* BERUFE UND ARBEITSWELT

der Arbeiter	worker, (industrial) labourer
der Architekt, -en	architect
der Bauunternehmer	builder, building contractor
der Bergarbeiter	miner
der Beruf, -e	profession, calling
der Bibliothekar, -e	librarian
Büroangestellte(r), -n	office worker
der Chef, -s	boss, head
der Elektriker	electrician
der Feuerwehrmann, (-männer)	fireman
der Fotograf, -en	photographer
der Fürst, -en	(reigning) prince
der Handwerker	tradesman
der Ingenieur, -e	engineer
der Journalist, -en	journalist
der Koch, ̈e	cook
der Kollege, -n	colleague
der König, -e	king
der Künstler	artist
der Last(kraft)wagenfahrer,	
der LKW-Fahrer	lorry driver
der Lehrer	teacher
der Matrose, -n	sailor
der Pfarrer	minister, clergyman
der Polizist, -en	policeman
der Präsident, -en	president
der Priester	priest
der Prinz, -en	prince
der Reporter	reporter
der Richter	judge
der Schriftsteller	author, writer
der Seemann, (-leute)	seaman
der Soldat, -en	soldier
der Star*, -s	star (*male or female*)
der Taxifahrer	taxi driver
der Verkäufer	salesman, assistant

* BERUFE UND ARBEITSWELT (*f*)

die Arbeit, -en	work; job
die Arbeiterin	worker
die Architektin	architect
die Bibliothekarin	librarian
die Chefin	boss
die Friseuse, -n	hairdresser
die Fürstin	(reigning) princess
die Journalistin	journalist
die Köchin	cook
die Kollegin	colleague
die Königin	queen
die Krankenschwester, -n	nurse
die Künstlerin	artist
die Lehrerin	teacher
die Polizistin	policewoman, WPC
die Prinzessin	princess
die Putzfrau, -en	cleaner, cleaning woman
die Sekretärin	secretary
die Stelle,* -n	job, post
die Stellung, -en	position, job
die Verkäuferin	salesgirl, saleswoman, assistant

* BERUFE UND ARBEITSWELT (*nt*)

das Einkommen	income
das Geschäft*, -e	business, trade
das Handwerk, -e	trade, craft

was sind Sie von Beruf? what is your job?
ich bin Elektriker von Beruf I am an electrician by trade *or* to trade
sich um eine Stelle bewerben to apply for a job
100 Pfund in der Woche verdienen to earn £100 per week
seinen Lebensunterhalt verdienen to earn one's living
eine Stelle antreten to start work *or* a new job
mit der Arbeit anfangen, zu arbeiten beginnen to start work, get down to work

** BERUFE UND ARBEITSWELT (m)

Abgeordnete(r), -n	M.P., member of parliament
der Arbeitslohn, ⸚e	wages
der Autor, -en	author
der Boß, -sse	boss
der Dichter	poet
der Dolmetscher	interpreter
der Fachmann, (-leute)	specialist, expert
der Geschäftsmann*, (-leute)	businessman
der Hausmeister*	caretaker; janitor
der Kaiser	emperor
der Lohn, ⸚e	pay, wages
der Maler	painter
der Mechaniker	mechanic
der Minister	(government) minister
der Ministerpräsident, -en	prime minister, premier
der Poet, -en	poet
der Politiker	politician
der Premierminister	prime minister, premier
der Produzent, -en	(film) producer
der Psychologe, -n	psychologist
der Rechtsanwalt, ⸚e	lawyer; solicitor; barrister
Staatsbeamte(r), -n	civil servant
der Staatsmann, (-männer)	politician; statesman
der Streik, -s	strike
Streikende(r), -n	striker
der Streit, -e	dispute
der Tischler	joiner, carpenter
der Vertreter	representative, rep
der Weingärtner,	vinegrower, vineyard
der Winzer	owner
der Wirtschaftsprüfer	accountant

streiken to strike, be on strike
in Streik treten to go on strike
im Streik sein to be on strike

** BERUFE UND ARBEITSWELT (f)

die Ausbildung	training
die Bezahlung, -en	pay
die Dolmetscherin	interpreter
die Empfangsdame, -n	receptionist
die Firma, Firmen	firm
die Kaiserin	empress
die Laufbahn, -en	career
die Lohnerhöhung, -en	wage increase
die Platzanweiserin	usherette
die Psychologin	psychologist
die Rechtsanwältin	lawyer; solicitor; barrister
die Schneiderin	dressmaker
die Sprechstunden-hilfe, -n	(medical *etc*) receptionist
die Staatsbeamte, -n	civil servant
die Streikende, -n	striker
die Verwaltung, -en	administration
die Zukunft	future

** BERUFE UND ARBEITSWELT (nt)

das Gehalt, ⸚er	salary
das Interview, -s	interview
das Mannequin, -s	model
das Ministerium, -ien	(government) ministry

*** BERUFE UND ARBEITSWELT *(m)*

der **Ansager**	announcer
die **Arbeitslosen** *(pl)*	the unemployed
der **Astronaut, -en**	astronaut
der **Betriebsleiter**	manager; managing director
der **Bummelstreik, -s**	go-slow
der **Chirurg, -en**	surgeon
der **Fensterputzer**	window cleaner
der **Geschäftsführer**	executive; manager
der **Gewerkschaftsführer**	union leader
Handlungs-reisende(r), -n	(commercial) traveller, travelling salesman
der **Herzog, -e**	duke
der **Kameramann, (-männer)**	cameraman
der **Kanzler**	chancellor
der **Klempner**	plumber
der **Landstreicher**	tramp
der **Lehrling, -e**	apprentice; trainee
leitende(r) Angestellte(r), -n -n	executive
der **Leiter***	manager
der **Mönch, -e**	monk
der **Rennfahrer**	racing driver
der **Schornsteinfeger**	(chimney) sweep
der **Steinmetz, -en**	mason
der **Techniker**	technician, engineer
der **Tierarzt, ⁻e**	veterinary surgeon, vet
der **Verleger**	publisher
der **Wissenschaftler**	scientist

arbeitslos sein to be out of work, be unemployed
seine Stelle verlieren to lose one's job, be made redundant
jemanden entlassen to make somebody redundant, dismiss somebody
entlassen werden to get the sack, be sacked
Arbeitslosengeld beziehen, stempeln gehen to be on the dole, draw unemployment benefit

*** BERUFE UND ARBEITSWELT (f)

die **Ansagerin**	announcer
die **Astronautin**	astronaut
die **Chirurgin**	surgeon
die **Geschäftsführerin**	manageress
die **Geschäftsreise, -n**	business trip
die **Gewerkschaft, -en**	trade union
die **Lehrzeit, -en**	apprenticeship
die **Maschinen-**	
schreiberin	typist
die **Nonne, -n**	nun
die **Stenotypistin**	shorthand typist
die **Tierärztin**	veterinary surgeon, vet
die **Wissenschaftlerin**	scientist

auf (einer) Geschäftsreise sein to be (away) on a business trip

ehrgeizig ambitious

* EISENBAHN (m)

der Ausgang, ¨e	exit
der Bahnhof, ¨e	station
der Bahnhofsvorsteher	stationmaster
der Bahnsteig, -e	platform
der Bahnübergang, ¨e	level crossing
der Eingang, ¨e	entrance
der Fahrkarten- schalter	ticket office, booking office
der Fahrplan, ¨e	timetable
der Fahrpreis, -e	fare
der (Gepäck)träger*	porter
der Koffer	case, suitcase
der Lokomotivführer	train driver
der Platz*, ¨e	seat
der Reisende(r), -n	traveller
der (Reise)paß* -pässe	passport
der Reservierungs- schalter	booking office
der Schaffner	guard; ticket collector
der Wagen*	carriage, coach
der Wartesaal, (-säle)	waiting room
der Zug*, ¨e	train

* EISENBAHN (nt)

das Abteil, -e	compartment
das Fahrgeld, -er	fare
das Gepäck	luggage
das Gepäcknetz, -e	luggage rack
das Nichtraucher- abteil, -e	no-smoking compart- ment, non-smoker
das Raucherabteil, -e	smoking compartment
das (Reise)ziel, -e	destination (of person)
das Taxi, -s	taxi

auf dem Bahnhof at the station
der Zug fährt ein the train enters the station
der Zug fährt ab the train leaves the station
Erster-/Zweiter-Klasse Abteil first-class/second-class compartment

* EISENBAHN *(f)*

die Abfahrt, -en	departure
die Ankunft, ⸚e	arrival
die Auskunft* ⸚e	information desk *or* office
die Bahnlinie, -n	railway line
die Bestimmung, -en	destination *(of goods)*
die Bremse, -n	brake
die Brücke*, -n	bridge
die Eisenbahn, -en	railway
die Fahrkarte, -n	ticket
die Fahrt*, -en	journey
die Gepäckaufbewahrung(sstelle)	left-luggage office
die Klasse, -n	class
die Leitung, -en	direction
die Nummer, -n	number
die Reise*, -n	journey
die Reisende, -n	traveller
die Richtung, -en	direction
die Sperre, -n	barrier
die Strecke*. -n	(section of) railway line *or* track
die U-Bahn, -en *(die Untergrundbahn)*	underground (railway), subway

** EISENBAHN *(nt)*

das Gleis, -e	track; platform

mit der Bahn by rail
einfache (Fahr)karte single ticket
Rückfahrkarte return ticket
nach Bonn einfach a single to Bonn
nach Bonn und zurück a return to Bonn
die Fahrkarte knipsen to punch the ticket
packen to pack; auspacken to unpack
das Gepäck vom Gepäcknetz herunterheben to take
down the luggage from the rack
jemanden zum Bahnhof begleiten to go with somebody to the station

** EISENBAHN (m)

der **Anhänger***	label
der **Anschluß, –üsse**	connection
der **Aufkleber**	sticker, label
der **D-Zug, ⸚e**	through or fast train
(**Durchgangszug**)	(long-distance)
der **Eilzug, ⸚e**	express train (inter-city)
der **Gepäckwagen**	luggage van
der **Güterzug, ⸚e**	goods train
der **Inter-City-Zug, ⸚e**	(first-class) inter-city train
der **Kofferkuli, –s**	luggage trolley
der **Liegewagen**	couchette
der **Personenzug, ⸚e**	slow train
der **Pfiff, –e**	whistle (blast), signal
der **Schlafwagen**	sleeping car, sleeper
der **Schnellzug, ⸚e**	fast train, express train
der **Speisewagen**	dining car
der **U-bahnhof, ⸚e**	underground or subway
(der **Untergrundbahnhof**)	station

*** EISENBAHN (m)

der **Bestimmungsort**	destination (of goods)
der **Dienstwagen**	guard's van
der **Eisenbahner**	railwayman
der **Heizer**	fireman, stoker
der **(Schnell)imbiß, –sse**	snack bar
der **Taxistand, ⸚e**	taxi stand, taxi rank
der **Vorortzug, ⸚e**	commuter train

alles einsteigen! all aboard!
(in den Zug) einsteigen to get (up) into the train
(aus dem Zug) aussteigen to get off the train
umsteigen to change trains
den Zug erreichen or **erwischen** to catch the train
den Zug verpassen to miss the train
den Anschluß verpassen to miss one's connection
ist dieser Platz besetzt/frei?, ist hier besetzt/frei?
  is this seat taken/free?
hier ist besetzt this seat is taken

** EISENBAHN *(f)*

die Abteiltür, -en	carriage door
die Bahnhofsgast-	
stätte, -n	station buffet
die (Eisenbahn)-	
schienen *(pl)*	rails
die Haltestelle, -n	minor station *or* stop
die Notbremse, -n	alarm, communication cord
die Schranke, -n	level crossing gate
die U-bahnstation,	
-en *(die Unter-*	
grundbahnstation)	underground station, subway station

*** EISENBAHN *(f)*

die Entgleisung, -en	derailment
die Kiste, -n	trunk
die Lokomotive, -n	locomotive, engine
die Monatskarte/	
Wochenkarte, -n	monthly/weekly season ticket
die Rolltreppe, -n	escalator

der Kopf/das Ende des Zuges the front/back of the train

der Personenzug von/nach München the slow train from/to Munich

'nicht hinauslehnen' 'do not lean out of the window'

entgleisen to be derailed

die Notbremse ziehen to pull the communication cord

Vorsicht am Gleis 3, der Zug von München fährt in Kürze ein 'the Munich train will shortly be arriving at platform 3'

Kurswagen through carriage *or* coach

* FAHRRAD *(m)*

der Gang*, ¨e	gear
der Radfahrer	cyclist
der (Rad)reifen	tyre
der Sattel, ¨	saddle, seat

** FAHRRAD *(m)*

der Berg*, -e	slope
der Dynamo, -s	dynamo
der Gepäckträger*	luggage rack
der Korb*, ¨e	pannier
der Radsport	cycling

*** FAHRRAD *(m)*

der Rad(fahr)weg, -e	cycle track
der Rückstrahler	reflector

* FAHRRAD *(nt)*

das Fahrrad, ¨er	bicycle
das Pedal, -e	pedal
das Rad*, ¨er	wheel; bike
das Radfahren	cycling

** FAHRRAD *(nt)*

das Hinterrad, ¨er	rear wheel
das Schutzblech, -e	mudguard
das Vorderrad, ¨er	front wheel

*** FAHRRAD *(nt)*

das Flickzeug, -e	puncture repair kit
das Katzenauge, -n	reflector

mit dem (Fahr)rad fahren, radeln to cycle
'Radfahren verboten' 'cycling prohibited'
radfahren to ride a bicycle, go cycling
Radsport betreiben to go in for cycling
er kam mit dem Rad he came on his bike *or* by bike
  mit dem Rad in die Stadt fahren, in die Stadt
  radeln to go to town by bike, to cycle to town
eine Radtour machen to go for a bike ride

* **FAHRRAD** (f)

die Bremse, -n	brake
die Fahrradlampe, -n	lamp
die Geschwindigkeit, -en	speed
die Kette*, -n	chain
die Lampe, -n	lamp
die Pumpe, -n	pump
die Radfahrerin	cyclist
die Reifenpanne, -n	puncture

** **FAHRRAD** (f)

die Klingel, -n	bell
die Lenkstange, -n	handlebars
die Satteltasche, -n	saddlebag

*** **FAHRRAD** (f)

die Gangschaltung, -en	gear-change
die (Rad)nabe, -n	hub
die (Rad)speiche, -n	spoke
die Stange*, -n	crossbar
die Steigung, -en	gradient

(auf das Rad) aufsteigen to get onto one's bike
(vom Rad) absteigen to get off one's bike
ein geplatzter Reifen a burst tyre
ein platter Reifen a flat tyre
einen Platten haben to have a flat tyre
ein Loch (im Reifen) flicken to mend a puncture
die Reifen aufpumpen to blow up the tyres
(mit dem Rad) bergauf/bergab fahren to go *or*
  cycle uphill/downhill
mit Freilauf fahren to freewheel
schalten to change gear
mit höchster Geschwindigkeit at full *or* top speed
plötzlich bremsen to brake suddenly
die Bremsen versagten the brakes failed
klingeln to ring one's bell
rostig rusty; glänzend shiny

* FAHRZEUGE (m)

der Bus, -se	bus
der Hubschrauber	helicopter
der Kinderwagen	pram
der Krankenwagen	ambulance
der Lastwagen,	
der LKW (Lastkraft-	
wagen)	lorry, truck
der Lieferwagen	(delivery) van
der Omnibus, -se	bus
der (Reise)bus, -se	coach
der Transporter	van
der Wagen*	car; cart
der Wohnwagen	caravan
der Zug*, ¨e	train

* FAHRZEUGE (f)

die Autofähre, -n	car ferry
die Fähre, -n	ferry(-boat)
die Straßenbahn, -en	tram

reisen to travel
eine Reise machen to go on a journey
mit der Bahn or dem Zug fahren or reisen to go or
  travel by rail or train
den Zug nehmen to take the train
das Flugzeug nach Köln nehmen to go to Cologne
  by air or by plane
nach Köln fliegen to fly to Cologne
mit dem Auto fahren to go by car, to drive
zu Fuß gehen to go on foot
mit dem (Fahr)rad fahren to go by bike, to cycle
mit dem Schiff fahren to go by boat, to sail
sie fuhren mit dem Schiff nach Australien they
  sailed to Australia
per Anhalter fahren, trampen to hitch-hike
rufen Sie einen Krankenwagen! call an ambulance!

* FAHRZEUGE (*nt*)

das **Auto**, -s	car
das **Boot**, -e	boat
das **Düsenflugzeug**, -e	jet plane
das **Fahrgeld**, -er	fare
das **Fahrrad**, ¨er	bicycle
das **Flugzeug**, -e	plane, aeroplane
das **Mofa**, -s	moped (*small*)
das **Moped**, -s	moped
das **Motorrad**, ¨er	motorcycle, motorbike
das **Rad***, ¨er	bike
das **Ruderboot**, -e	rowing boat
das **Schiff***, -e	ship; vessel
das **Taxi**, -(s)	taxi

** FAHRZEUGE (m)

der Bulldozer	bulldozer
der Dampfer	steamer
der Fahrpreis, -e	fare
der Karren	cart
der Möbelwagen	removal van
der Motorroller	scooter
der Personendampfer	passenger steamer, liner
der Sattelschlepper	articulated lorry
der Straßenbahn-wagen	tramcar
der Vergnügungs-dampfer	pleasure steamer

** FAHRZEUGE (f)

die **Drahtseilbahn, -en**	cable car (on rails), funicular (railway)
die **Düse, -n**	jet (plane)
die **Jacht, -en**	yacht
die **Planierraupe, -n**	bulldozer
die **Rakete, -n**	rocket
die **Schwebebahn, -en**	cable car

** FAHRZEUGE (nt)

das **Beiboot, -e**	lifeboat (from ship)
das **Fährboot, -e**	ferry-boat
das **Fahrzeug, -e**	vehicle
das **Feuerwehrauto, -s**	fire engine
das **Kanu, -s**	canoe
das **Motorboot, -e**	motorboat
das **Paddelboot, -e**	canoe
das **Rettungsboot, -e**	lifeboat
das **Schlauchboot, -e**	inflatable dinghy
das **Schnellboot, -e**	speedboat
das **Segelboot, -e**	sailing boat
das **Unterseeboot, -e,**	
das **U-Boot, -e**	submarine

ein Boot zu Wasser lassen to launch a boat
eine Rakete starten to launch a rocket
wie eine Rakete davonschießen to shoot off like a rocket
bootfahren gehen to go boating
paddeln gehen to go canoeing
rudern gehen to go rowing
segeln gehen, zum Segeln gehen to go sailing

*** FAHRZEUGE (m)

der Anhänger*	trailer
der Flugzeugträger	aircraft carrier
der Frachtkahn, ⸚e	barge
der Jeep, -s	jeep
der Kombiwagen	estate car
der Lastkahn, ⸚e	barge
der (Luft)ballon, -s or -e	balloon
der Panzer	tank
der Schleppdampfer,	
der Schlepper	tug
der Sessellift, -e or -s	chair-lift
der Tanker	tanker

*** FAHRZEUGE *(f)*

die fliegende Unter- tasse, -n -n	flying saucer
die grüne Minna	Black Maria
die Lokomotive, -n	locomotive, engine

*** FAHRZEUGE *(nt)*

das Flugzeugmutter- schiff, -e	aircraft carrier
das Luftkissen- fahrzeug, -e	hovercraft
das Luftschiff, -e	airship
das Raumschiff, -e	spaceship
das Schleppschiff, -e	tug
das Segelflugzeug, -e	glider
das Tankschiff, -e	tanker
das Transportmittel	means of transport *(for goods)*
das Verkehrsmittel	means of transport *(for passengers)*
das Wasserflugzeug, -e	seaplane

öffentliche Verkehrsmittel *(pl)* public transport

* FAMILIE (m)

Alte(r), -n	old man
der Bräutigam, -e	bridegroom; fiancé
der Bruder, ∶	brother
die Eltern (pl)	parents
der Enkel	grandson
die Enkel (pl)	grandchildren
die Geschwister (pl)	brothers and sisters
der Großvater, ∶	grandfather
der Jugendliche	youth (person)
die Jugendlichen (pl)	young people, youths
der Junge, -n	boy
der junge Mann	youth, young man
die Jungverheirateten (pl)	newly-weds
die Leute (pl)	people
der Mann*, Männer	man; husband
die Menschen (pl)	people, human beings
der Nachbar, -en	neighbour
der Name*, -n	name
der Onkel	uncle
der Sohn, ∶e	son
der Vater, ∶	father
Verwandte(r), -n	relation, relative
der Vetter	cousin

Mutti!, Mama! Mummy!; Vati!, Papa! Daddy!
der (or die) jüngste (in) der Familie the youngest
   in the family
der (or die) älteste (in) der Familie the oldest in
   the family
jünger als younger than; älter als older than
er ist gleich alt wie ich, er ist im gleichen Alter
   wie ich he is the same age as me
der Stammbaum the family tree
sein/ihr einziger Sohn his/her only son
seine/ihre einzige Tochter his/her only daughter
wie heißt er? what is his name?, what is he called?
er heißt Peter his name is Peter
ein Kind Paul nennen to call a child Paul

* FAMILIE (*f*)

die Braut, Bräute	bride; fiancée
die Enkelin	grand-daughter
die Familie, -n	family
die Frau*, -en	woman; wife
die Großmutter, ‥	grandmother
die Heirat, -en	marriage
die Hochzeit, -en	wedding
die Kusine, -n	cousin
die Mutter, ‥	mother
die Nachbarin	neighbour
die Person*, -en	person
die Schwester, -n	sister
die Tante, -n	aunt
die Tochter, ‥	daughter
die Verwandte, -n	relation, relative
die Verwandtschaft (sg)	relations, relatives

* FAMILIE (*nt*)

das Alter*	age; old age
das Baby, -s	baby
das Ehepaar, -e	married couple
das Enkelkind	grandchild
das Fräulein	young lady
das frischgebackene Ehepaar, -n -e	the newly-weds
das Kind, -er	baby, child, kid
das Mädchen	(young) girl
das Paar*, -e	couple
das Weib, -er	woman (*old-fashioned or pejorative*)

die Familie/das Kind **wächst** the family/the child
is growing
meine Eltern **werden alt** my parents are getting old
jemanden **kennenlernen**, jemandes **Bekanntschaft
machen** to meet somebody, get to know somebody
jemanden **heiraten** to marry somebody
sich verheiraten (mit) to get married (to)
wieder heiraten to remarry, get married again
verlobt engaged; **geschieden** separated; divorced

** FAMILIE (m)

der Cousin, -s	cousin
der Ehegatte, -n	spouse
der Ehemann, (-männer)	husband; married man
die Erwachsenen (pl)	grown-ups, adults
der Familienname, -n	surname
der Kleine, -n	kid, little one
der Mädchenname, -n	maiden name
der Nachname, -n	surname
der Neffe, -n	nephew
der Rufname, -n	first name, Christian name
der Säugling, -e	baby, infant
Verlobte(r), -n	fiancé
der Vorname, -n	first name, Christian name
der Zuname, -n	surname
die Zwillinge (pl)	twins
der Zwillingsbruder, ¨	twin brother

** FAMILIE (f)

die Hausfrau, -en	housewife
die Jugend	youth (stage of life)
die Kleine, -n	kid, little one
die Nichte, -n	niece
die Verlobte, -n	fiancée
die Zwillings- schwester, -n	twin sister

** FAMILIE (nt)

das Au-pair, -s	au pair
das Greisenalter, das hohe Alter	old age

in meiner Jugend in my youth
als ich jung war when I was young
bei den Schmidts at the Smiths'
meine Mutter geht arbeiten *or* geht zur Arbeit my
mother goes out to work

*** FAMILIE (m)

der Ahne, -n	ancestor
der Junggeselle, -n	bachelor
der Pate, -n	godfather
der Rentner	(old age) pensioner
der Schwager, "	brother-in-law
der Schwiegersohn, "e	son-in-law
der Schwiegervater, "	father-in-law
der Spitzname, -n	nickname
der Stammvater, "	ancestor
der Taufzeuge, -n	godfather
der Vorfahr, -en	ancestor
der Vormund, -e or "er	guardian
der Witwer	widower

*** FAMILIE (f)

die alte Jungfer, -n -n	spinster
die Patin	godmother
die Rentnerin	(old age) pensioner
die Schwägerin	sister-in-law
die Schwiegermutter, "	mother-in-law
die Schwiegertochter, "	daughter-in-law
die Waise, -n	orphan
die Witwe, -n	widow

*** FAMILIE (nt)

das ältere Fräulein	spinster, old maid
das Waisenhaus, "er	orphanage
das Waisenkind, -er	orphan

ein eingefleischter Junggeselle a confirmed bachelor

das Nesthäkchen in der Familie the baby of the family, the pet

mein Onkel ist Witwer/ist Rentner my uncle is a widower/is a pensioner

im Ruhestand sein to be retired

eine Mutter, die ihre Kinder verläßt a mother who abandons her children

ein Vater, der seine Kinder im Stich läßt a father who abandons his children

FARBEN

beige	beige
blau	blue
braun	brown
gelb	yellow
golden	golden
grau	grey
grün	green
karmesinrot,	
karminrot	crimson
orange	orange
purpurrot	scarlet
rehbraun	fawn
rosa	pink
rot	red
schwarz	black
silbern	silver
veilchenblau	violet
violett	purple
weiß	white
dunkelblau	dark blue
hellblau	pale blue
bläulich	bluish
himmelblau	sky blue
königsblau	royal blue
marineblau	navy blue

das Blau steht ihr blue suits her
etwas blau anstreichen to paint something blue

die Farbe wechseln to change colour
bunte/düstere Farben bright/dark colours
das Farbfernsehen colour television

FARBEN *(Forts)*

was für eine Farbe hat es? what colour is it?
das Weiße Haus the White House
ein Weißer, eine Weiße a white man, a white woman
schneeweiß as white as snow
Rotkäppchen Little Red Riding Hood
leichenblaß as white as a sheet, deathly pale
blau vor Kälte blue with cold
braun werden to go *or* turn brown *(of people, leaves)*
braun wie ein Haselnuß as brown as a berry
grün und blau black and blue
ein Schwarzer, eine Schwarze a black man, a black woman
ein blaues Auge a black eye
gelb vor Neid green with envy

* FISCHE UND INSEKTEN *(m)*

der Fisch, -e	fish
der Käfer	beetle
der Schwanz, ¨e	tail
der Schmetterling, -e	butterfly

** FISCHE UND INSEKTEN *(m)*

der Floh, ¨e	flea
der Flügel*	wing
der Goldfisch, -e	goldfish
der Hai(fisch), -e *and* (-e)	shark
der Hering, -e	herring
der Kabeljau, -e	cod
der Krebs, -e	crab
der Lachs, -e	salmon
der Marienkäfer	ladybird
der Moskito, -s	mosquito
der Nachtfalter	moth
der Weißfisch, -e	whiting
der Wurm, ¨er	worm

*** FISCHE UND INSEKTEN *(m)*

der Aal, -e	eel
der Hecht, -e	pike
der Hummer	lobster
der Thunfisch, -e	tuna fish, tunny fish
der Tintenfisch, -e	(small) octopus

*, ** FISCHE UND INSEKTEN *(nt)*

das Insekt, -en	insect
das Schalentier, -e	shellfish

fischen (gehen), zum Fischen gehen to go fishing
angeln gehen, zum Angeln gehen to go fishing *(with a line)*
ein Fisch hat angebissen I've got (*or* he's got) a bite
ein Fisch an der Angel haben to have a fish on the line
Schmetterlinge sammeln to collect butterflies
munter wie ein Fisch im Wasser as happy as a lark

* FISCHE UND INSEKTEN (*f*)

die Biene, -n	bee
die Fliege*, -n	fly
die Luft	air
die Spinne, -n	spider
die Wespe, -n	wasp

** FISCHE UND INSEKTEN (*f*)

die Ameise, -n	ant
die Forelle, -n	trout
die Grille, -n	cricket
die Krabbe, -n	shrimp; prawn
die (Mies)muschel, -n	mussel
die Motte, -n	(wool-eating) moth
die Mücke, -n	midge
die Wanze, -n	bug

*** FISCHE UND INSEKTEN (*f*)

die Auster, -n	oyster
die Flosse, -n	fin
die Kiemen (*pl*)	gills
die Krake, -n	octopus
die Libelle*, -n	dragonfly
die Qualle, -n	jellyfish
die Raupe, -n	caterpillar
die Schmeißfliege, -n	bluebottle
die Schuppe, -n	scale
die Seezunge, -n	sole
die Seidenraupe, -n	silkworm

schwimmen to swim; **fliegen** to fly
ein Spinnennetz (*nt*) a spider's web
Krabbencocktail (*m*) prawn cocktail
stechen to sting
die Wespe/die Biene sticht the wasp/bee stings

* AUF DEM FLUGHAFEN (m)

der Abflug, ⸚e	take-off, departure
der Absturz, ⸚e	air *or* plane crash
der Ausgang, ⸚e	exit; gate (*before boarding plane*)
der Eingang, ⸚e	entrance
der Fahrplan, ⸚e	timetable
der Fallschirm, -e	parachute
der Flug, ⸚e	flying; flight
der Fluggast, ⸚e	passenger
der Flughafen, ⸚	airport
der Flugplatz, ⸚e	airfield; airport
der Flugpreis, -e	(air) fare
der Gepäckträger*	porter
der Hubschrauber	helicopter
der Koffer	case, suitcase
der Notausgang, ⸚e	emergency exit
der Paß*, ⸚sse	passport
der Pilot, -en	pilot
Reisende(r), -n	traveller
der Reisepaß, ⸚sse	passport
der Tourist, -en	tourist
der Träger	porter
der Urlauber	holiday-maker
der Zoll	customs
Zollbeamte(r), -n	customs officer

packen to pack; **auspacken** to unpack
eine Flugkarte lösen to buy a ticket
einen Flug buchen to book a (one-way) flight
einen Rückflug buchen to book a return flight

* AUF DEM FLUGHAFEN (f)

die Ankunft, ⸚e	arrival
die Ausreise, -n	exit; departure (*from country*)
die Flughalle, -n	air terminal
die Flugkarte, -n	ticket
die Gepäckaufbewahrung(sstelle)	left-luggage office
die Geschwindigkeit	speed
die Luft	air
die Reisende, -n	traveller
die Touristin	tourist
die Urlauberin	holiday-maker
die Wartehalle, -n	(departure) lounge

* AUF DEM FLUGHAFEN (nt)

das Flugzeug, -e	plane, aeroplane
das Gepäck	luggage

** AUF DEM FLUGHAFEN (m)

der Anhänger*	label
der Anschluß, ¨sse	connection
der Aufkleber	sticker, label
der Flügel*	wing
der Geschäftsmann*,	
(-leute)	businessman
der Jumbojet, -s	jumbo jet
der Kofferkuli, -s	luggage trolley
der Sicherheitsgurt, ¨e	seat belt
der Start, -e	take-off
der Steward, -s	steward
der zollfreie Laden, -n ¨	duty-free shop

** AUF DEM FLUGHAFEN (f)

die Abfertigungshalle, -n	air terminal
die Ankunftshalle, -n	arrival lounge
die Besatzung, -en	crew
die Düse, -n	jet (plane)
die Einreisekarte, -n	landing card
die Höhe*	height
die Landebahn, -en	runway
die Landung, -en	landing; descent
die Rollbahn, -en,	
die Startbahn, -en	runway
die Stewardeß, -essen	air hostess

** AUF DEM FLUGHAFEN (nt)

das Abheben	take-off
das Düsenflugzeug, -e	jet plane
das Reiseziel, -e	destination
das zollfreie Geschäft, -n -e	duty-free shop

beim Start during (the) take-off
schnallen Sie sich bitte an, (on *notice*) 'Bitte
anschnallen' please fasten your seat belts
wir haben eine Flughöhe von ... we are flying at
a height of ...
wir setzen zur Landung an we are beginning our
descent

*** AUF DEM FLUGHAFEN (m)

der **Abstieg**	descent
der **Fluglotse, -n**	air traffic controller
der **Kontrollturm, ":e**	control tower
der **Luftsack, ":e**	air pocket; windsock
der **Radar**	radar
der **Rollsteg, -e**	moving pavement
der **Windsack, ":e**	windsock

*** AUF DEM FLUGHAFEN (f)

die **Flugleitung**	air traffic control
die **Luftkrankheit**	air sickness
die **Luftschraube, -n**	propeller
die **Luftverkehrs-**	
gesellschaft, -en	airline
die **Reservierung, -en**	reservation
die **Rolltreppe, -n**	escalator
die **Schallmauer**	sound barrier
die **Steuerung** (sg)	controls
die **Turbulenz**	turbulence
die **Zwischenlandung, -en**	stopover

*** AUF DEM FLUGHAFEN (nt)

das **Bodenpersonal**	ground staff
das **Fliegen**	flying
die **Landebahnfeuer** (pl)	runway lights
das **Luftloch, ":er**	air pocket
das **Radar**	radar
das **Reisebüro, -s**	travel agency
das **Ruder*** (sg)	controls

beim Abstieg fiel der Motor aus the engine failed during the descent
die Schallmauer durchbrechen to break the sound barrier
ein Überschallflugzeug (nt) a supersonic plane
durch den Zoll gehen to go through customs
haben Sie etwas zu verzollen? do you have anything to declare?
nichts zu verzollen nothing to declare

* GARTEN UND BLUMEN (m)

der Ast, ¨e	branch
der Baum, Bäume	tree
der Baumstamm, ¨e	tree trunk
der Blumenstrauß, (-sträuße)	bunch of flowers; bouquet of flowers
der Boden*, ¨	earth, ground, soil
der Busch, ¨e	bush, shrub
der Duft, ¨e	perfume, scent
der Garten, ¨	garden
der Gärtner	gardener
der Gemüsegarten, ¨	vegetable garden, kitchen garden
der Grund*, ¨e	ground; soil
der Obstgarten, ¨	orchard
der Pfad, -e	path
der Rasen	lawn, turf
der Schatten	shadow
der Schmetterling, -e	butterfly
der Stamm, ¨e	trunk
der Stein, -e	stone, rock
der Strauß*, Sträuße	bunch (of flowers)
der Weg*, -e	path
der Zweig, -e	branch

den Garten umgraben to dig the garden
Blumen pflanzen to plant flowers
die Blumen wachsen the flowers grow
blühen to blossom; pflücken to pick
den Rasen mähen to mow the lawn
ein Strauß Rosen/Veilchen, ein Rosenstrauß/
  Veilchenstrauß a bunch of roses/violets

* GARTEN UND BLUMEN *(f)*

die Beere, -n	berry
die Biene, -n	bee
die Blume, -n	flower
die Butterblume, -n	buttercup
die Erde, -n	earth, soil, ground
die Hecke, -n	hedge
die Margerite, -n	daisy
die Pflanze, -n	plant
die Pforte, -n	(garden) gate
die Rose, -n	rose
die Tulpe, -n	tulip
die Walze, -n	roller
die Wespe, -n	wasp

* GARTEN UND BLUMEN *(nt)*

das Blatt, ⁻er	leaf
das Gärtnern	gardening
die Gemüse *(pl)*	vegetables
das Gras	grass

** GARTEN UND BLUMEN *(nt)*

das Gänseblümchen	daisy
das Gartenhaus, (-häuser)	summerhouse
das Gewächshaus, (-häuser)	greenhouse
das Laub(werk) *(sg)*	leaves, foliage
das Maiglöckchen	lily of the valley
das Samenkorn, (-körner)	a seed
das Unkraut *(sg)*	weed(s)
das Veilchen	violet
das Werkzeug, -e	tool

der Garten ist von einer Hecke umgeben the garden is surrounded by a hedge
der Garten ist umzäunt the garden is fenced in
das duftet *or* **riecht gut** that smells nice
das riecht schlecht that smells nasty
im Schatten eines Baumes in the shade of a tree
im Schatten bleiben to remain in the shade *or* in the shadows

** GARTEN UND BLUMEN (m)

der Dorn, -en	thorn
der Efeu	ivy
der Flieder	lilac
der Hahnenfuß (sg)	buttercup
der Krokus, - or -se	crocus
der Mohn, -e	poppy
der Rasenmäher	lawnmower
der Rosenstock, ¨e,	
der Rosenstrauch,	
(-sträucher)	rose bush
der Samen	seed
der Schaft, ¨e	stalk
der Schubkarren	wheelbarrow
der Stachel, -n	thorn
der Wurm, ¨er	worm
der Zaun, Zäune	fence

** GARTEN UND BLUMEN (f)

die Blüte	blossom
die Chrysantheme, -n	chrysanthemum
die Dahlie, -n	dahlia
die (Garten)bank*, ¨e	(garden) seat
die Gießkanne, -n	watering can
die Hacke*, -n	hoe
die Harke, -n	rake
die Hütte*, -n	hut, shed
die Hyazinthe, -n	hyacinth
die Knospe, -n	bud
die Lilie, -n	lily
die Narzisse, -n	narcissus, daffodil
die Nelke, -n	carnation
die Osterglocke, -n	daffodil
die Sonnenblume, -n	sunflower

die Hecke schneiden or **stutzen** to cut or trim the hedge
die Blumen gießen to water the flowers
den Garten jäten, jäten to weed the garden, do the weeding

*** GARTEN UND BLUMEN (m)

der Goldlack (sg)	wallflower
der Halm, -e	stalk, stem
der Löwenzahn (sg)	dandelion
der Schlauch, Schläuche	garden hose
der Steingarten, ⸚	rockery, rock garden
der Stengel,	
der Stiel, -e	stalk, stem
der Strauch, Sträucher	shrub
der Tau	dew
der Weiher	pond, small lake

*** GARTEN UND BLUMEN (f)

die Gartenlaube, -n	summerhouse
die Heckenschere, -n	hedge-cutters, garden shears
die Laube, -n	summerhouse
die Orchidee, -n	orchid
die Primel, -n	primrose
die Rabatte, -n	border
die Wurzel, -n	root

*** GARTEN UND BLUMEN (nt)

das Blumenbeet, -e	flowerbed
das Geißblatt	honeysuckle
das Schneeglöckchen	snowdrop
das Stiefmütterchen	pansy
das Vergißmeinnicht, -e	forget-me-not

hacken to hoe the ground
die Blätter zusammenharken to rake up the leaves
ein sonniges/schattiges Plätzchen a sunny/shady spot
sich mit der Hand an einem Dorn reißen to scratch one's hand on a thorn
eine Blume im Knopfloch tragen to wear a buttonhole

* GEMÜSE *(m)*

der **Blumenkohl**, -e	cauliflower
der **grüne Salat**, -n -e	lettuce; green salad
der **Kohl**, -e	cabbage
der **(Kopf)salat**, -e	lettuce
der **Spinat**	spinach

** GEMÜSE *(m)*

der **Champignon**, -s	(button) mushroom
der **eßbare Pilz**, -n -e	mushroom
der **Knoblauch**	garlic
der **Lauch**, -e	leek
der **Pilz**, -e	mushroom
der **Porree**, -s	leek
der **Rosenkohl** *(sg)*	Brussels sprouts
der **Spargel**	asparagus

*** GEMÜSE *(m)*

der **Gartenkürbis**, -se	marrow
der **Kürbis**, -se	pumpkin
der **Mais**	sweet corn
der **Maiskolben**	corn on the cob
der **Paprika** *(sg)*	pepper (red, green)
der **Rettich**, -e	(large) radish
der **Sellerie**	celeriac
der **Stangensellerie**	celery

*, ** GEMÜSE *(nt)*

das **Gemüse**	vegetable
das **Kraut**	cabbage
das **Radieschen**	(red) radish
das **Sauerkraut**	pickled cabbage

Gemüse **anbauen** to grow vegetables
2 Krautköpfe, 2 Kohle 2 cabbages
Kräuter herbs
eine Knoblauchzwiebel a head of garlic
eine Knoblauchzehe a clove of garlic
Knoblauchwurst *(f)* garlic sausage
den Salat **umheben** to toss the salad

* GEMÜSE (f)

die Bohne, -n	bean
die Erbse, -n	pea
die Gurke, -n	cucumber
die Karotte, -n	carrot
die Kartoffel, -n	potato
die Möhre, -n,	
die Mohrrübe, -n	carrot
die Tomate, -n	tomato
die Zwiebel, -n	onion

** GEMÜSE (f)

die Essiggurke, -n	gherkin
die Petersilie	parsley
die Rübe, -n	turnip

*** GEMÜSE (f)

die Artischocke, -n	artichoke
die Aubergine, -n	aubergine
die Brunnenkresse	watercress
die Eierfrucht, ⁻e	aubergine
die Endivie, -n	endive
die Erdartischocke, -n	Jerusalem artichoke
die Kresse	cress
die Paprikaschote, -n	pepper (red, green)
die rote Rübe, -n -n	beetroot

grüne Bohnen French beans
eine Bohnenstange beanpole (literal and figurative)
junge Erbsen garden peas
Salzkartoffeln boiled potatoes (peeled)
Pellkartoffeln, Schalkartoffeln boiled potatoes in
their jackets
geraspelte Möhre grated carrot
rot wie eine Tomate as red as a beetroot
ich esse gern Bohnen I like beans
ich mag keine Bohnen, ich mag Bohnen nicht I
don't like beans

GEOGRAPHISCHE EIGENNAMEN—ORTE

Antwerpen *(nt)*	Antwerp
der **Ärmelkanal**	the English Channel
der **Atlantik,**	
der **Atlantische Ozean**	the Atlantic (Ocean)
Basel *(nt)*	Basle
Bayern *(nt)*	Bavaria
der **Bodensee**	Lake Constance
die **britischen Inseln**	
(*fpl*)	the British Isles
Brüssel *(nt)*	Brussels
die **Donau**	the Danube
Edinburg *(nt)*	Edinburgh
Elsaß *(nt)*	Alsace
der **Ferne Osten**	the Far East
Genf *(nt)*	Geneva
der **Genfer See**	Lake Geneva
Gent *(nt)*	Ghent
der **Große Ozean**	the Pacific Ocean
Den Haag *(nt)*	the Hague
Hannover *(nt)*	Hanover
Kairo *(nt)*	Cairo
die **Kanalinseln** (*fpl*)	the Channel Islands
Köln *(nt)*	Cologne
Korsika *(nt)*	Corsica
Lissabon *(nt)*	Lisbon
Lothringen *(nt)*	Lorraine
Mailand *(nt)*	Milan
Mallorca *(nt)*	Majorca
das **Mittelmeer**	the Mediterranean
die **Mosel**	Moselle
Moskau *(nt)*	Moscow
München *(nt)*	Munich
der **Nahe Osten**	the Near East
die **Nordsee**	the North Sea
der **Pazifik,**	
der **Pazifische Ozean**	the Pacific (Ocean)
die **Pyrenäen** *(pl)*	the Pyrenees
der **Rhein**	the Rhine
Rom *(nt)*	Rome

GEOGRAPHISCHE EIGENNAMEN—ORTE

der Schwarzwald	the Black Forest
die Seine	the Seine
der Stille Ozean	the Pacific Ocean
die Themse	the Thames
Venedig (*nt*)	Venice
der Vesuv	Mount Vesuvius
Warschau (*nt*)	Warsaw
Wien (*nt*)	Vienna
die Wolga	the Volga

GEOGRAPHISCHE EIGENNAMEN —PERSONEN

Athener, -in an Athenian
Bas(e)ler, -in a person from Basle
Bayer, -in a Bavarian
Böhme, Böhmin a person from Bohemia
Elsässer, -in a person from Alsace, an Alsatian
Flame, Flamin *or* **Flämin** a person from Flanders, a Fleming
Friese, Friesin a person from Frisia, a Frisian
Hamburger, -in a person from Hamburg
Hannoveraner, -in a person from Hanover, a Hanoverian
Hesse, Hessin a person from Hesse
Indianer, -in a (Red) Indian
Londoner, -in a Londoner
Moskauer, -in a person from Moscow, a Muskovite
Münch(e)ner, -in a person from Munich
Neapolitaner, -in a Neapolitan
Pariser, -in a Parisian
Preuße, Preußin a Prussian
Rheinländer, -in a Rheinlander
Römer, -in a person from Rome, a Roman
Sachse, Sächsin a person from Saxony
Schwabe, Schwäbin a person from Swabia
Tiroler, -in a person from the Tyrol
Venezianer, -in a Venetian
Westfale, Westfälin a Westphalian
Wiener, -in a person from Vienna, a Viennese

* GESCHÄFTE UND GESCHÄFTSLEUTE (m)

der **Apotheker**	(dispensing) chemist
der **Artikel**	article; (selling) line
der **Bäcker**	baker
der **Buchhändler**	bookseller
der **Drogist, -en**	retail chemist
der **Fleischer**	butcher
der **Juwelier**	jeweller
der **Kaufmann, (-leute)**	merchant
der **Konditor, -en**	confectioner; pastry-cook, baker
der **Kunde, -n**	customer, client
der **Laden***, ⏜	shop
der **Ladentisch, -e**	counter (*in shop*)
der **Lebensmittelhändler**	grocer
der **Markt, ⏜e**	market
der **Metzger**	butcher
der **Obsthändler**	fruiterer
der **Preis*** -e	price
der **Schalter**	counter (*in post office, bank etc*)
der **Supermarkt, ⏜e**	supermarket
der **Süßwarenver-käufer**	confectioner, sweetshop owner
der **Tabakladen**, ⏜	tobacconist's (shop)
der **Verkäufer**	salesman, shop assistant

am Markt, auf dem Markt in *or* at the market
Einkäufe machen to do some shopping
einkaufen gehen, zum Einkaufen gehen to go shopping
etwas kaufen/verkaufen to buy/sell something
an der Kasse bezahlen to pay at the cash desk
was *or* **wieviel kostet es?** how much is it?
das macht 70 Pfennig that's 70 Pfennigs (in all)
ich habe 5 Mark dafür bezahlt I paid 5 marks for it
das ist zu teuer that is too dear
das ist sehr billig that is very cheap
das ist preiswert that is good value, that is worth the money

* GESCHÄFTE UND GESCHÄFTSLEUTE (f)

die Apotheke, -n	dispensing chemist's, pharmacy
die Bäckerei, -en	bakery
die Bank*, -en	bank
die Bibliothek, -en	library
die Bücherei, -en	(lending) library
die Buchhandlung, -en	bookshop, bookseller's
die Drogerie, -n	(retail) chemist's
die Firma, Firmen	firm, company, business
die Fleischerei, -en	butcher's (shop)
die Gesellschaft, -en	company
die Kasse, -n	till; cash desk
die Konditorei, -en	cake shop, confectioner's
die Kundin	customer, client
die Metzgerei, -en	butcher's shop
die Post*, -en	post office
die Rechnung, -en	bill
die Reinigung	dry cleaner's
die Schlange*, -n	queue
die Theke, -n	counter (in café, bar etc)
die Tierhandlung, -en	pet shop
die Verkäuferin	salesgirl, shop assistant

beim Fleischer, in der Fleischerei at the butcher's
einen Scheck ausstellen/einlösen to write/cash a cheque
mit Scheck bezahlen to pay by cheque
bar bezahlen to pay cash
auf der Bank Geld abheben to withdraw *or* take out money from the bank
Schlange stehen to queue (up)
GmbH Ltd.

* GESCHÄFTE UND GESCHÄFTSLEUTE *(nt)*

das Büro, -s	office
das Café, -s	café
das Erdgeschoß, -sse	ground floor
das Erzeugnis, -se	product; produce
das Geld	money
das Geschäft*, -e	shop; deal; trade, business
das Geschenk, -e	present, gift
das Kaufhaus, (-häuser)	large shop, department store; warehouse
das Kellergeschoß, -sse	basement
das Kleingeld	(small) change
das Lebensmittel-geschäft, -e	grocer's, general food store
das Milchgeschäft, -e	dairy
das Postamt, ¨er	post office
das Produkt, -e	product; produce
das Restaurant, -s	restaurant
das Schaufenster	shop window
das Süßwaren-geschäft, -e	confectioner's, sweetshop
das Warenhaus, (-häuser)	department store, general store

im Erdgeschoß on ground level, on the ground floor
im Kellergeschoß in the basement
zu viel verlangen to be asking too much
zu viel Geld ausgeben to spend too much money
Schaufenster anschauen, einen Schaufenster-
 bummel machen to go window-shopping
'zum Verkauf' 'for sale'

** GESCHÄFTE UND GESCHÄFTSLEUTE (m)

der Einkauf, (-käufe)	shopping; purchase, thing bought
der Fischhändler	fishmonger
der Friseur, -e	hairdresser
der Geschäftsmann*, (-leute)	trader, businessman
der Grundstücks- makler	estate agent
der Händler	dealer
der Herrenfriseur, -e	barber, men's hairdresser
der Juwelier	jeweller
der Käufer	buyer
der Obst- und Gemüsehändler	greengrocer
der Scheck, -s	cheque
der Schneider	tailor
der Schlußverkauf, (-käufe)	(end-of-season) sale
der Uhrmacher	watchmaker
der Verkauf, (-käufe)	sale
der Zeitungshändler	newsagent

** GESCHÄFTE UND GESCHÄFTSLEUTE (f)

die Farbe*, -n	colour
die Friseuse, -n	hairdresser
die Gaststätte, -n	restaurant
die Größe*, -n	size
die Kleiderpuppe, -n	dummy, model
die Kneipe, -n	pub
die Kragenweite	collar size
die Schaufenster- puppe, -n	dummy, model
die Sparkasse, -n	savings bank
die Versicherung- (sgesellschaft), -en	insurance company

** GESCHÄFTE UND GESCHÄFTSLEUTE *(nt)*

das Einkaufen	shopping
das Juweliergeschäft, -e	jeweller's (shop)
das Reisebüro, -s	travel agency
das Schuhgeschäft, -e	shoe shop
das Wechselgeld	change *(after buying)*
das Wirtshaus, (-häuser)	pub; inn

*** GESCHÄFTE UND GESCHÄFTSLEUTE *(nt)*

das Gewerbe	trade, business, line
das Parterre, -s	ground floor
das Schreibwarengeschäft, -e	stationer's
das Sonderangebot, -e	bargain (offer), special offer
das Textilgeschäft, -e	draper's (shop)

Waren liefern to deliver goods
ausverkauft! sold out!
garantieren, gewährleisten to guarantee
eine Garantie auf etwas geben to guarantee something

*** GESCHÄFTE UND GESCHÄFTSLEUTE (m)

der Buchmacher	bookmaker, 'bookie'
der Eisenwarenhändler	ironmonger
der (Flick)schuster	cobbler, shoe repairer
der Gelegenheitskauf, (-käufe)	bargain (purchase)
der Handel	trade, business
der Optiker	optician
der Schuhmacher	shoemaker, shoe repairer
der Waschsalon, -s	laundrette

*** GESCHÄFTE UND GESCHÄFTSLEUTE (f)

die Baugenossenschaft, -en	building society
die Besorgung, -en	errand
die Bude, -n	stall
die Eisenwarenhandlung, -en	ironmonger's, hardware shop
die Filiale, -n	branch
die Garantie, -n	guarantee
die Parfümerie, -n	perfume counter or shop
die Quittung, -en	receipt
die Rabattmarke, -n	trading stamp
die Schuhgröße, -n	shoe size
die Wäscherei, -en	laundry, cleaner's

* GESUNDHEIT (m)

der Apotheker	(dispensing) chemist
der Arzt, ⸚e	doctor, physician, G.P.
der Husten	cough
die Kopfschmerzen (pl)	a headache
der Krankenpfleger	(male) nurse
der Krankenwagen	ambulance
Kranke(r), -n,	
der Patient, -en	patient
der Schmerz, -en	pain, ache; (pl) grief
der Schock	shock
der Verband, ⸚e	bandage, dressing
der Zahnarzt, ⸚e	dentist

* GESUNDHEIT (f)

die Ärztin	doctor, physician, G.P.
die Bandage, -n	elastic bandage
die Erkältung, -en	cold; chill
die Gesundheit	health
die Grippe	flu, influenza
die Kraft, ⸚e	strength, power
die Kranke, -n	patient
die Krankenschwester, -n	nurse
die Krankheit, -en	illness
die Medizin	(science of) medicine
die Patientin	patient
die Pille, -n	pill
die Salbe, -n	ointment, cream
die Tablette, -n	tablet, pill
die Temperatur, -en	temperature
die Verletzung, -en	injury
die Wunde, -n	wound
die Zahnärztin	dentist

krank ill, sick; wohl well; gesund healthy; nicht
wohl off colour; geschwollen swollen
sich fühlen, sich befinden to feel, be; leiden (an
+ dat) to suffer (from); verordnen to prescribe
heilen to cure; genesen, sich erholen to recover;
versorgen to look after

* **GESUNDHEIT** *(nt)*

das **Aspirin**	aspirin
das **Blut**	blood
das **Fieber**	fever, (high) temperature
das **Kopfweh**	headache
das **Krankenhaus**, (-häuser)	hospital
das **Pflaster**	sticking plaster
das **Rezept***, -e	prescription
das **Sprechzimmer**	surgery, consulting room

** **GESUNDHEIT** *(m)*

der **Atem**	breath
der **Atemzug**, ¨e	a breath; *(pl)* breathing
die **Bauchschmerzen** *(pl)*	stomach-ache
der **Bazillus**, Bazillen	germ
der **Gipsverband**, ¨e	plaster (cast)
die **Halsschmerzen** *(pl)*	a sore throat
der **Heuschnupfen**	hayfever
der **Hitzschlag**	heatstroke
der **Kratzer**	scratch
die **Magenschmerzen** *(pl)*	stomach-ache
der **Mumps**	mumps
der **Nerv**, -en	nerve
der **Operationssaal**, (-säle)	(operating) theatre
der **Puls**	pulse
der **Rollstuhl**, ¨e	wheelchair
der **Schnupfen**	cold (in the head)
der **Schweiß**	sweat
der **Sonnenstich**	sunstroke
der **Stich**, -e	sting
die **Zahnschmerzen** *(pl)*	toothache

in die **Praxis kommen** to come to the surgery
was **fehlt** Ihnen? what's the matter with you?
sich *(dat)* **weh tun** to hurt oneself
sich **verletzen** to injure oneself
er ist auf dem **Weg der Besserung** he is getting
  better; gute **Besserung!** get well soon!
ansteckend contagious, infectious

** GESUNDHEIT (f)

die Armbinde, -n	sling
die Blase, -n	blister; bladder
die Blinddarmentzündung	appendicitis
die Epidemie, -n	epidemic
die Erste Hilfe	first aid
die Injektion, -en	injection
die Klinik, -en	hospital, clinic
die Krücke, -n	crutch
die Mandelentzündung	tonsillitis
die Narbe, -n	scar
die Oberschwester, -n	matron
die Operation, -en	operation
die Poliklinik, -en	health centre
die Röntgenaufnahme, -n	X-ray
die Ruhe*	rest
die Schiene, -n	splint
die Station, -en	ward
die Tragbahre, -n	stretcher
die Übelkeit	sickness, vomiting
die Untersuchung*	medical examination
die Zunge, -n	tongue

** GESUNDHEIT (nt)

das Erbrechen	sickness, vomiting
das Gift	poison
das Halsweh	sore throat
das Zahnweh	toothache

sich den Arm brechen to break one's arm
im Bett bleiben to stay in bed
ruhen, sich ausruhen to rest, have a rest
stöhnen; ächzen (vor + *dat*) to groan (with)
in Ohnmacht fallen, ohnmächtig werden to faint
ohne Bewußtsein unconscious; das Bewußtsein
verlieren to lose consciousness; wieder zum
Bewußtsein kommen to regain consciousness
außer Atem out of breath; atemlos breathless
schwach weak; geschwächt weakened
mit aller Kraft with all one's strength

*** GESUNDHEIT (m)

der Herzanfall, ∵e	heart attack
der Keuchhusten	whooping cough
der Rückfall, ∵e	relapse
der Schlaganfall, ∵e	stroke
der Typhus	typhoid
der Zustand, ∵e	state, condition

*** GESUNDHEIT (f)

die Abmagerungskur	(slimming) diet
die Blutübertragung	blood transfusion
die Diät	(special) diet
die Droge, -n	drug
die Genesung	recovery
die Leiche, -n	corpse
die Masern (pl)	measles
die Migräne	migraine
die Pocken (pl)	smallpox
die Röteln (pl)	German measles
die Spritze, -n	injection, jag, jab
die Watte	cotton wool
die Windpocken (pl)	chickenpox

*** GESUNDHEIT (nt)

das Altersheim, -e	old folks' home
das Antiseptikum	antiseptic
das Leiden	complaint, condition
das Mittel*	remedy
das Rauschgift, -e	drug, narcotic
das Schwindelgefühl	giddiness

ich bin erkältet, ich habe eine Erkältung I've got a cold

(erhöhte) Temperatur haben to have a temperature

Fieber haben to have a high temperature

husten to cough; niesen to sneeze; den Schluckauf haben to have hiccoughs

sich übergeben, erbrechen to vomit, be sick

dabei wird mir übel or schlecht it makes me feel sick

GRÜSSE UND ABSCHIEDSGRÜSSE
GREETINGS AND FAREWELLS

guten Tag good day, hello; good afternoon
guten Morgen good morning
guten Abend good evening, good night
gute Nacht good night (*when going to bed*)
auf Wiedersehen goodbye
auf Wiederhören goodbye (*on phone*)
he! hi!; Tschüs! bye!
wie geht's?; wie geht es Ihnen? how are you?
gut, danke; es geht mir gut, danke very well, thank you
sehr angenehm pleased to meet you
bis später see you later
bis morgen see you tomorrow

GLÜCKWÜNSCHE   BEST WISHES

ich gratuliere! congratulations!
alles Gute all the best, best wishes
herzliche Glückwünsche congratulations, best wishes
alles Gute zum Geburtstag happy birthday
alles Gute zum Hochzeitstag congratulations on your wedding day
viel Glück all the best; the best of luck
fröhliche Weihnachten merry Christmas
gutes neues Jahr happy New Year
guten Appetit, gesegnete Mahlzeit have a good meal, enjoy your meal
prosit! cheers!; zum Wohl! good health!
Gesundheit! bless you! (*after a sneeze*)
viel Spaß! have a good time, enjoy yourself *etc*
schlaf gut! sleep well
gut geschlafen? did you sleep well?
ausgeschlafen? did you have a good sleep?

grüßen, begrüßen to greet, welcome
sich verabschieden to say goodbye, take one's leave
(sich) vorstellen to introduce (oneself)

ÜBERRASCHUNG   SURPRISE

ach du meine Güte oh my goodness, oh dear
so?, wirklich? really?
so, so! well, well! **ach so!** oh I see!
na, so etwas! you don't say!
wie? what?
was für (eine Menge Leute)! what (a crowd)!
was für ein Glück! what a piece of luck!, how
   fortunate!

HÖFLICHKEITSFORMELN   POLITENESS

bitte please, excuse me
danke thank you; **nein danke** no thank you
ja bitte, bitte ja yes please
bitte nicht! no, please don't!
tu das ja nicht don't do that
danke schön, danke sehr, vielen Dank thank you
   very much, many thanks
bitte schön, bitte sehr don't mention it
gern geschehen my pleasure, don't mention it
entschuldigen Sie, Entschuldigung excuse me; I'm
   sorry
verzeihen Sie, Verzeihung (*formal*) I'm sorry, I beg
   your pardon
pardon excuse me, I'm sorry
es macht nichts it doesn't matter
(wie) bitte? (I beg your) pardon?
na bitte, bitte schön, bitte sehr there you are
mit Vergnügen with pleasure
machen Sie keine Umstände don't go to any trouble

WARNUNGEN   WARNINGS

Achtung! watch out!; **Vorsicht!** be careful!
paß auf! look out!, watch out!
halten Sie! stop!
Feuer! fire!; **haltet den Dieb!** stop thief!
sei ruhig! be quiet!; **halt den Mund!** shut up!
herein! come in!; **heraus!** get out!
beeile dich! hurry up!; **hau ab!** clear off!
geh mir aus dem Weg! get out of my way!

ZUSTIMMUNG UND ABLEHNUNG
AGREEMENT AND DISAGREEMENT

ja yes; **doch** yes (*when contradictory*)
nein no
jawohl yes indeed
natürlich of course
natürlich nicht, aber nein of course not
nicht wahr? isn't that right?
in Ordnung O.K., all right
gut good, O.K.
na gut, also gut O.K. then, all right then
schön fine
einverstanden! agreed!
genau, ganz recht exactly
desto besser so much the better
ich habe nichts dagegen I don't mind *or* object
das ist mir gleich *or* **einerlei** *or* **egal** I don't mind,
  it's all the same to me, it's all one to me
das stimmt that's right
das stimmt nicht that doesn't make sense
im Gegenteil on the contrary
nie!, um nichts in der Welt! never!, not on your
  life!
kümmern Sie sich um Ihre eigenen Dinge mind
  your own business
nieder mit ... down with ...

UNANGENEHME SITUATIONEN   DISTRESS

Hilfe! help!
ach je! oh dear!
ach!, o weh! alas!
was ist los (mit dir)? what's the matter (with you)?,
 what's wrong (with you)?
leider (nicht) unfortunately (not)
es tut mir leid I'm sorry
es tut mir wirklich leid I'm really sorry
wie schade what a pity
das ist Pech it's a shame, that's bad luck
verflixt (nochmal)! blow!, drat!, dash it!
verflucht!, verdammt! damn!
ich habe es satt I'm fed up with it
ich kann ihn nicht ausstehen I can't stand him
was soll ich tun? what shall I do?
es ist unnütz or **nutzlos, das zu tun** there's no use
 doing that
wie ärgerlich! what a nuisance!, how annoying!

ANDERE AUSDRÜCKE   OTHERS

vielleicht perhaps, maybe
ich weiß nicht I don't know
(ich habe) keine Ahnung (I've) no idea
ich weiß da nicht Bescheid I don't know (anything
 about it)
ich weiß nicht genau I don't know exactly
das kann ich mir vorstellen I can believe that
Schade! shame!
mein Gott! good Lord!
(ach) du lieber Himmel! (good) heavens!, goodness
 gracious!
prima! great!
klasse! terrific!, marvellous!
machen Sie sich keine Sorgen don't worry
aber wirklich! well really!
du machst wohl Witze you must be joking or kidding
so eine Frechheit what a nerve or cheek
armes Ding! poor thing!

* HAUS *(m)*, **≠**

der Boden*, ≠	floor
der Flur, -e	corridor; entrance hall
der Fußboden	floor
der Gang*, ≠e	corridor; landing
der Hausmeister*	caretaker
der Hausrat *(sg)*	household goods
der Kamin, -e	chimney; fireplace
der Keller	basement; cellar
der Korridor, -e	corridor; hall
der Nachbar, -n	neighbour
der Rauch	smoke
der Raum*, Räume	room; space
der Schlüssel	key
der Schornstein*, -e	chimney
der Stock, Stockwerke	floor, storey
der Wohnblock, -s	block of flats

* HAUS *(nt)*

das Bad*(ezimmer), ≠er *and* (-)	bathroom
das Dach, ≠er	roof
das Erdgeschoß, -sse	ground floor
das Eßzimmer	dining room
das Etagenhaus	flat
das Fenster	window
das Geschoß, -sse	floor, storey
das Haus, Häuser	house
das Kaminsims, -e	mantelpiece
das Kellergeschoß, -sse	basement
das Klosett, -e	toilet
die Möbel *(pl)*	furniture
das Möbel(stück)	piece of furniture
das Schlafzimmer	bedroom
das Speisezimmer	dining room
das Stockwerk, -e	floor, storey
das Treppenhaus	staircase
das Untergeschoß, -sse	basement
das Wohnzimmer	lounge, living room
das Zimmer	room

* HAUS (f)

die Bequemlichkeit	comfort
die Dachstube, -n	attic
die Decke*, -n	ceiling
die Diele, -n	hall
die Einrichtung	furnishings
die Etagenwohnung, -en	flat
die Familie, -n	family
die Garage, -n	garage
die Hausfrau, -en	housewife
die Haustür, -en	front door
die Kellerwohnung, -en	basement flat
die Küche, -n	kitchen
die Mansarde, -n	attic
die Mauer, -n	(outside) wall
die Nachbarin	neighbour
die Putzfrau, -en,	
die Reinmachefrau, -en	cleaning woman
die Toilette, -n	toilet
die Treppe, -n	stairs, staircase
die Tür, -en	door
die Wand, ¨e	(inside) wall
die Wohnung, -en	flat

in einer Wohnung wohnen to live in a flat
im ersten/zweiten Stock on the first/second floor
im Untergeschoß, im Kellergeschoß in the basement
im Erdgeschoß on the ground floor, on ground level
zu Hause, daheim at home
ein Haus bauen to build a house, have a house built
oben upstairs; unten downstairs; die Treppe hinauf/hinunter gehen to go upstairs/downstairs
bis zur Decke up to the ceiling
ein Zimmer betreten, in ein Zimmer (ein)treten to go into a room
zum Fenster hinaussehen, aus dem Fenster sehen to look out of the window
schön (her)gerichtet well decorated

** HAUS (m)

der Balkon*, -s	balcony
der Laden*, ¨	shutter
der Mieter	tenant
der Parkettfußboden	wooden or parquet floor
der Riegel	bolt
der Rolladen, ¨	blind
der Umzug, ¨e	removal

** HAUS (f)

die Antenne, -n	aerial
die Fensterscheibe, -n	window pane
die Glastür (-en) nach draußen	French window
die Jalousie, -n	(venetian) blind
die Miete, -n	rent
die Stube, -n	sitting room, parlour
die Stufe, -n	step
die Türklingel, -n	doorbell
die Verandatür, -en	French window
die Zentralheizung	central heating

** HAUS (nt)

das alleinstehende Haus, -n Häuser	detached house
das Arbeitszimmer	study
das Doppelhaus, (-häuser)	semi-detached (house)
das Gästezimmer,	
das Gastzimmer,	spare room, guest room
das Gebäude	building
das Parkett*, -e	wooden or parquet floor
das Rollo, -s, das Rouleau, -s	blind
das Schloß*, ¨sser	lock
das Studierzimmer	study

umziehen to move (house); einziehen to move in
in eine andere Stadt ziehen to move to another town
sich einleben to settle down, settle in

*** HAUS (m)

der Abstellraum	box room
der Boiler	boiler
der Bungalow, -s	bungalow
der Dachziegel	roof tile
der Etagenabsatz, ⸚e	landing
der Fensterladen, ⸚	shutter
der (Fenster)sims, -e	window ledge *or* sill
der Putz	plaster
der Speiseschrank, ⸚e	larder
der Treppenabsatz, ⸚e	landing
der Verputz	plaster

*** HAUS (f)

die Dachrinne, -n	gutter
die Fassade, -n	front (*of house*)
die Fliese, -n	(floor) tile
die Front, -en	front (*of house*)
die Fußbodenfliese, -n	(floor) tile
die Haustürstufe, -n	doorstep
die Hütte*, -n	cottage
die Kachel, -n	(wall) tile
die Rumpelkammer	junk room
die Scheidewand, ⸚e	partition, dividing wall
die Schieferplatte, -n	slate
die Speisekammer, -n	larder
die Trennwand, ⸚e	partition
die (Tür)stufe, -n	doorstep

*** HAUS (nt)

das Abflußrohr, -e	drainpipe
das Dachfenster	skylight
das Fensterbrett, -er	window ledge
das (Fenster)sims, -e	window ledge *or* sill
das Oberlicht, -er	skylight

an die Tür klopfen to knock at the door
es hat geklopft somebody knocked (at the door)
es hat (an der Tür) geklingelt, jemand hat geklingelt the doorbell rang, somebody rang the doorbell

* HAUSHALT (*m*)

der Abfall	rubbish, refuse
der Besen	broom
der Briefkasten, ⸚	letterbox
der Deckel	lid
der Fernsehapparat, -e,	
der Fernseher	television set
der Griff, -e	handle (*of door etc*)
der Handbesen,	
der Handfeger	brush
der Henkel	handle (*of jug etc*)
der Kamm, ⸚e	comb
der Küchenabfall	refuse
der Kühlschrank, ⸚e	fridge
der Lappen,	
der Lumpen	rag
der Müll	rubbish, refuse
der Pinsel*	paintbrush; brush
der Schmutz	dirt
der Schrank, ⸚e	cupboard
der Spiegel	mirror
der Staubsauger	vacuum cleaner, hoover
der Stiel, -e	handle (*long*)
der Teppich, -e	rug
der Wecker	alarm clock
der Wischlappen	duster

die Hausarbeit machen to do the housework
das Geschirr spülen to wash the dishes
spülen, abwaschen to do the washing-up
waschen to do the washing
bügeln to do the ironing
kehren, fegen to sweep
reinigen, putzen to clean, do the cleaning
abstauben to dust, do the dusting
staubsaugen to hoover, do the vacuuming
der Frühjahrsputz the spring cleaning
seine Sachen aufräumen to tidy up one's things
seine Sachen überall herumliegen lassen to leave
  one's things lying about everywhere

* HAUSHALT (f)

die Badewanne, -n	bath
die Bürste, -n	brush
die Dusche, -n	shower
die Elektrizität	electricity
die Hausarbeit	housework
die Klinke, -n	(door) handle
die Leiter, -n	ladder
die Sachen (pl)	things
die Seife	soap
die Stielkasserolle, -n	pan, saucepan
die Wanne, -n	bath
die Zahnbürste, -n	toothbrush
die Zahncreme, die Zahnpasta	toothpaste

* HAUSHALT (nt)

das Abwaschtuch, ¨er	dish cloth
das Bild, -er	picture, painting
das Brett*, -er	tray
das Bügeleisen	iron
das Gas	gas
das Geschirrtuch, ¨er	dish cloth; tea towel
das Handtuch, ¨er	(hand) towel
das Rezept*, -e	recipe
das Spülbecken	sink
das Staubtuch, ¨er	duster
das Tablett, -e,	tray
das Teebrett, -er	tray
das Waschbecken	washbasin
das Wasser	water

** HAUSHALT (m)

der Papierkorb, ¨e	waste paper basket
der Spüllappen	dish cloth
der Spültisch, -e	sink unit
der Staub	dust
der Toaströster	toaster
der Topf, ¨e	pot
der Vorleger	rug, mat

** HAUSHALT (f)

die Bettdecke, -n	blanket, cover
die Bratpfanne, -n	frying pan
die Brücke*, -n	(narrow) rug or mat
die Farbe*	paint; colour
die Kaffeemühle, -n	coffee grinder
die Pfanne, -n	frying pan
die Rührmaschine, -n	(electric) mixer
die Spüle, -n	sink unit
die Tapete	wallpaper
die Vase, -n	vase
die (Woll)decke*, -n	blanket

** HAUSHALT (nt)

das Gemälde	painting, picture
das Kissen	cushion; pillow
das Kopfkissen	pillow
das Polster	cushion; pillow
das Reinmachen	cleaning
das Schampoon	shampoo
das Seifenpulver	soap powder

*** HAUSHALT (nt)

das Bettlaken,	sheet
das Bettuch, ̈er	sheet
das Bügelbrett, -er	ironing board or table
das Laken,	
das Leintuch, ̈er	sheet
das Rohr, -e	pipe

baden, ein Bad nehmen to take a bath
sich im Spiegel betrachten to look at oneself in the mirror
etwas in einer Pfanne zubereiten or braten to cook something in a pan
Zwiebeln anbraten to fry onions
das Wasser läuft in das (Spül)becken the water flows or runs into the sink
etwas in den Mülleimer werfen to throw something in the dustbin

*** HAUSHALT (*m*)

der Aschenbecher	ashtray
der Bettvorleger	bedside rug
der Eimer	bucket
der Fön, -e	hair-drier
der Hahn*, ⸚e	tap
der Kachelofen, ⸚	tiled stove
der Kessel	kettle
der Kleiderbügel	coat hanger
der Kohleneimer,	
der Kohlenkasten, ⸚	coal scuttle
der Krug, ⸚e	jug
der Mixer	(electric) blender
der Mülleimer	dustbin
der Rasierapparat, -e	razor
der Rasierpinsel	shaving brush
der Schalter	switch
der Schneebesen	whisk, egg beater
der Schürhaken	poker
der Schwamm, ⸚e	sponge
der Teppichkehrer	carpet sweeper
der Ziergegenstand, ⸚e	ornament

*** HAUSHALT (*f*)

die Daunendecke, -n	eiderdown
die Fußmatte, -n	doormat
die Heizdecke, -n	electric blanket
die Kanne, -n	jug
die Matte, -n	rug
die Nackenrolle, -n	bolster
die Rasierklinge, -n	razor blade
die Röhre, -n,	
die Rohrleitung, -en	pipe
die Steppdecke, -n	(continental) quilt
die Teppichkehr- maschine, -n	carpet sweeper
die Trockenhaube, -n	hair-drier
die Waage, -n	(set of) scales
die Wärmflasche, -n	hot water bottle
die Wäscheschleuder, -n	spin dryer

* HOBBYS (m)

der Anfänger	beginner
der Ausflug, ⸚e	outing, trip
der Film, -e	film
der Freund, -e	friend; boyfriend
der Jugendklub, -s	youth club
der Kanal*, Kanäle	(TV) channel
der Kassettenrecorder	cassette recorder
der Nachtklub, -s	night club
der (Photo)apparat, -e,	
der Photo, -s	camera
der Plattenspieler	record player
der (Pop)sänger	(pop) singer
der Roman, -e	novel
der Spaziergang, ⸚e	walk
der Tanz, ⸚e, der	
Tanzabend, -e	dance
der Wettbewerb, -e	competition
der Zeitvertreib, -e	pastime

* HOBBYS (nt)

das Ferienlager	school camp
das Feriendorf, ⸚er	holiday camp
das Fernsehen	television
das Hobby, -s	hobby
das Interesse, -n	interest
das Kino, -s	cinema
das Kreuzworträtsel	crossword (puzzle)
das Lied, -er	song
das Mitglied, -er	member
das Museum, Museen	museum
das Picknick, -e or -s	picnic
das Programm, -e	(TV) programme; (TV) channel
das Radio, -s	radio
das Singen	singing
das Taschengeld	pocket money
das Transistorradio	transistor (radio)
das Wandern	hiking, rambling
das Wochenende	weekend

---

* HOBBYS (f)

die Anfängerin	beginner
die Ausstellung, -en	exhibition
die Begeisterung	enthusiasm
die Diskothek, -en	discotheque
die Einladung, -en	invitation
die Freizeit	spare time, free time
die Freundin	friend; girlfriend
die Nachrichten (pl)	news, newscast
die Party, -s	party
die Photo(graphie), -s and (-n)	photo(graph)
die Photographie	photography
die (Pop)musik	pop music
die (Pop)sängerin	(pop) singer
die Reise*, -n	trip, journey
die Sammlung, -en	collection
die (Schall)platte, -n	record
die Sendung, -en	transmission, broadcast
die (Spiel)karte, -n	(playing) card
die Versammlung, -en	meeting, gathering
die Wanderung, -en	hike, ramble
die Zeitschrift, -en	magazine

am Wochenende at the weekend
in meiner Freizeit in my spare time
amüsiere dich gut! enjoy yourself!
es hat mir wirklich gut gefallen I really enjoyed
  myself
sich langweilen, Langeweile haben to be bored
faulenzen to laze about or around
ich gehe gerns ins Kino I like going to the cinema
mir macht Briefmarkensammeln Spaß I like
  collecting stamps
Briefmarken tauschen to swap stamps
Karten/Schach/Damen spielen to play cards/chess/
  draughts
sich für klassische Musik etc interessieren to be
  interested in classical music etc
sportinteressiert sein to be interested in sport

** HOBBYS *(m)*

der Brieffreund, -e	penfriend
der Chor, -̈e	choir
der Fan, -s	fan
der Fortsetzungs-roman, -e	serial
der Krimi, -s	thriller, detective story
der Pfadfinder	boy scout
der Song, -s	folk song, blues song

** HOBBYS *(f)*

die Brieffreundin	penfriend
die Briefmarksamm-lung, -en	stamp collection
die Hitparade	hit parade
die Langspielplatte, -n, die LP	LP
die Langeweile	boredom
die Malerei, -en	painting
die Oper, -n	opera; opera house
die Pfadfinderin	girl guide
die Schlagerparade	hit parade
die (Schmal)film-kamera, -s	cine camera
die Theatergruppe, -n	drama group, dramatic society

** HOBBYS *(nt)*

das Album, Alben	album (*for stamps etc*)
das Band*, -̈er	(recording) tape
das Damespiel	draughts
das Gemälde	painting, picture
das Kartenspiel, -e	game of cards
das LP-Album, (-Alben)	album, LP
das Modell, -e	model
das Nähen	sewing
das Plattenalbum, (-alben)	record
das Schachspiel, -e	game of chess; chess set
das Stricken	knitting
das (Ton)band, -̈er	tape
das Verein, -e	club

*** HOBBYS (m)

der Abzug, ¨e	(photographic) print, copy
der Bastler	handyman, do-it-yourselfer
der Musikautomat, -en	jukebox
der Spielautomat, -en	slot machine

*** HOBBYS (f)

die Pfadfinderei	scouting; guiding
die Stickerei	embroidery
die Töpferei	pottery (hobby)

*** HOBBYS (nt)

das Bridge	bridge (game)
das Dia(positiv), -s and (-e)	slide, (colour) transparency
das Do-it-yourself	do-it-yourself, DIY
das Pfadfindertum	scouting; guiding

spazieren gehen, einen Spaziergang machen to go for a walk
im Fernsehen on television
fernsehen to watch television
umschalten to turn over, change programmes
Radio hören to listen to the radio
Platten hören to play records, listen to records
eine (Schall)platte auflegen to put on a record
jemanden/etwas photographieren to take photos of somebody/something
stricken/nähen to do one's knitting/sewing
im Chor singen to sing in the choir
wir kommen jeden Freitag zusammen we meet every Friday
seine Zeit (damit) verbringen, etwas zu tun to spend one's time doing something

* IM HOTEL (m)

der Aufzug, ¨e	lift
der Empfangschef, -s	receptionist, reception clerk
der Gast, ¨e	guest
der Gastwirt, -e	innkeeper; host
der Gepäckträger*	porter
der Kellner	waiter
der Koch, ¨e	cook
der Koffer	case, suitcase
der Küchenchef, -s	chef, head cook
der Lift, -e or -s	lift
der Ober	waiter
der Pensionär, -e	resident, guest (in guest-house etc)
der Stock, Stockwerke	floor, storey
der Wirt, -e	innkeeper; host

ein Zimmer in einem Hotel bestellen to book a room in a hotel
ein Einzelzimmer a single room
ein Doppelzimmer a double room
ein Zimmer mit Doppelbett a twin-bedded room
(ein) Zimmer mit Dusche/mit Bad (a) room with a shower/with private bathroom
was kostet es?, wie teuer ist es? how much is it?
im ersten/zweiten Stock on the first/second floor
im Erdgeschoß on the ground floor, on ground level
Herr Ober! waiter!
Fräulein! waitress!, excuse me, miss!

* IM HOTEL (f)

die Aussicht	view
die Bar, -s	bar
die Bedienung	service; service charge
die Dusche, -n	shower
die Empfangsdame, -n	receptionist
die Garderobe*, -n	cloakroom
die Gastwirtin	innkeeper; innkeeper's wife
die Kellnerin	waitress
die Köchin	cook
die Pension*, -en	guest-house, boarding house
die Rechnung, -en	bill
die Rezeption	reception, reception desk
die Wirtin	innkeeper's wife

* IM HOTEL (nt)

das Badezimmer	bathroom
das (Farb)fernsehen	(colour) television
das Gepäck	luggage
das Hotel, -s	hotel
das Restaurant, -s	restaurant
das Schwimmbecken	swimming pool
das Speisezimmer	dining room
das Stockwerk, -e	floor, storey
das Trinkgeld, -er	tip
das Wirtshaus, (-häuser)	pub; inn
das Zimmer	room

** IM HOTEL (m)

der Balkon*, -s *or* -e	balcony
der Fernsehraum, (-räume)	television *or* TV lounge
der Hotelier	hotelier, hotel-keeper
der Page, -n	page(-boy)
der Weinkellner	wine waiter

*** IM HOTEL (m)

der Notausgang, ¨e	emergency exit
der Oberkellner	head waiter
der Zuschlag, ¨e	supplement

** IM HOTEL (f)

die Empfangshalle, -n	foyer
die Gaststätte, -n	restaurant
die Terrasse, -n	terrace
die Trinkstube, -n	bar (*room*)
die Vorhalle, -n	foyer

*** IM HOTEL (f)

die Kneipe, -n	pub
die Schenke, -n	pub, bar

, * IM HOTEL *(nt)*

das **Café**, -s	café
das **Doppelbett**, -en	double bed
das **Doppelzimmer**	double room; twin-bedded room
das **Einzelzimmer**	single room
das **Foyer**	foyer
das **Freibad**, ̈er	open-air swimming pool
das **Gasthaus**, (-häuser)	inn; pub
das **(Klein)geld**	(small) change
das **Wechselgeld**	change *(after buying)*
Zimmer mit Frühstück	room *or* bed and breakfast
Zimmer mit Halbpension	(room with) half-board; bed, breakfast and evening meal
Zimmer mit Vollpension	(room with) full board
das **Zimmermädchen**	chambermaid

sich anmelden to register
ein Formular ausfüllen to fill in a form
'Bedienung inbegriffen' 'service included'
sein Gepäck auf *or* **in sein Zimmer bringen** to take up one's luggage to one's room
sein Gepäck aus seinem Zimmer herunterbringen to take down one's luggage from one's room
man hat mein Gepäck hinaufgetragen/hinuntergetragen they took up/took down my luggage (for me)
'Sie brauchen nur zu klingeln' 'just ring'
das Zimmer hat Aussicht *or* **Blick auf den Strand** the room overlooks the beach
das Zimmermädchen macht die Betten und reinigt die Zimmer the chambermaid makes the beds and cleans the rooms

* JUWELEN, SCHMUCK UND KOSMETIK *(m)*

der Armreif(en), -e *and* (-)	bracelet, bangle
der Diamant, -en	diamond
der Ring, -e	ring
der Spiegel	mirror

* JUWELEN, SCHMUCK UND KOSMETIK *(f)*

die Armbanduhr, -en	(wrist) watch
die Halskette, -n	necklace
die Kette*, -n	chain
die Kosmetik *(sg)*	cosmetics, make-up
die Perle, -n	pearl; bead

* JUWELEN, SCHMUCK UND KOSMETIK *(nt)*

das Armband, ¨er	bracelet
das Gold	gold
das Juwel, -en	jewel; *(pl)* jewels, jewellery
das Silber	silver

** JUWELEN, SCHMUCK UND KOSMETIK *(m)*

der Edelstein, -e	jewel
der Ohrring, -e	earring
der Rubin, -e	ruby
der Saphir, -e	sapphire
der Schatz, ¨e	treasure
der Schmuck, -e	jewellery
der Schönheitssalon	beauty salon
der Smaragd, -e	emerald

sich zurechtmachen, Make-up auflegen to make oneself up
sich waschen to have a wash, get washed
sich frisieren to do one's hair
sich die Haare bürsten to brush one's hair
sich (die Haare) kämmen to comb one's hair
sich rasieren to shave
sich im Spiegel betrachten to look at oneself in the mirror
sich *(dat)* die Fingernägel lackieren to varnish one's nails

** JUWELEN, SCHMUCK UND KOSMETIK (f)

die Brosche, -n	brooch
die Frisur, -en	hairstyle
die Krone, -n	crown
die Perlenkette, -n	beads, string of beads

** JUWELEN, SCHMUCK UND KOSMETIK (nt)

das Make-up	foundation; make-up
das Parfüm, -s or -e	perfume, scent
das Tempotaschentuch, ¨er	(paper) tissue
das Toilettenwasser	toilet water

*** JUWELEN, SCHMUCK UND KOSMETIK (m)

der Anhänger*	pendant
der Ehering, -e	wedding ring
der Halsreif, -e	choker
der Gesichtspuder	face powder
der Lidschatten	eye shadow
der Lippenstift	lipstick
der Lockenwickler	curler, roller
der Manschettenknopf, ¨e	cufflink
der Nagellack(ent- ferner)	nail varnish (remover)
der Trauring, -e	wedding ring

*** JUWELEN, SCHMUCK UND KOSMETIK (f)

die Gesichtscreme	face cream
die Krawattennadel	tie-pin
die Perücke, -n	wig
die Tiara	tiara
die Wimperntusche	mascara

*** JUWELEN, SCHMUCK, KOSMETIK (nt)

das Deodorant(spray) -s and (-s)	deodorant

kostbar precious
wertvoll valuable; wertlos worthless
echt real, genuine

KALENDER

DIE JAHRESZEITEN *(fpl)*

der Frühling	spring
der Sommer	summer
der Herbst	autumn
der Winter	winter

im Frühling/Sommer/Herbst/Winter in spring/summer/autumn/winter

DIE MONATE *(mpl)*

Januar	January	**Juli**	July
Februar	February	**August**	August
März	March	**September**	September
April	April	**Oktober**	October
Mai	May	**November**	November
Juni	June	**Dezember**	December

im September *etc* in September *etc*
der erste April April Fools' Day
der erste Mai May Day
der fünfte November (*Tag der Pulververschwörung in England*) Guy Fawkes Night

DIE TAGE *(mpl)* **DER WOCHE**

Montag	Monday
Dienstag	Tuesday
Mittwoch	Wednesday
Donnerstag	Thursday
Freitag	Friday
Samstag **Sonnabend** }	Saturday
Sonntag	Sunday

Freitags *etc* on Fridays *etc*
am Freitag *etc* on Friday *etc*
nächsten/letzten Freitag *etc* next/last Friday *etc*
am nächsten Freitag *etc* the following Friday *etc*

KALENDER

Palmsonntag	Palm Sunday
Ostersonntag	Easter Sunday
Ostermontag	Easter Monday
Pfingstmontag	Whit Monday
Fastnachtsdienstag	Shrove *or* Pancake Tuesday
Aschermittwoch	Ash Wednesday
Himmelfahrt(stag *m*) *f*	Ascension Day
Gründonnerstag	Maundy Thursday
Karfreitag	Good Friday
Allerseelen	All Souls' Day
Dreikönigsfest	Epiphany, Twelfth Night
Neujahr(stag)	New Year's Day
Advent	Advent
Allerheiligen	All Saints' Day, All Hallows' Day
Abend *m* vor Allerheiligen	Hallowe'en
Faschingszeit	the Fasching festival, carnival-time
Fastenzeit	Lent
Ostern	Easter
Passahfest	Passover
Pfingsten	Whitsun
Silvester (*nt*), Silvesterabend (*m*)	New Year's Eve, Hogmanay
Valentinstag	St Valentine's Day
Weihnachten (*pl*)	Christmas
Weihnachtsabend	Christmas Eve
Weihnachtstag	Christmas Day
zweiter Weihnachtsfeiertag	Boxing Day

zu Ostern/Pfingsten/Weihnachten at Easter/Whitsun/Christmas

KALENDER—BESONDERE EREIGNISSE

die Beerdigung	funeral, burial
die Bescherung (sg)	(distribution of) Christmas presents
der Feiertag	holiday
das Festival	festival
der Festtag	holiday
das Feuer im Freien	bonfire
das Feuerwerk	firework display
der Feuerwerkskörper	firework
der Friedhof	cemetery, churchyard
der Geburtstag	birthday
das Geschenk	present
die Heirat	marriage
der Hochzeitstag	wedding day
das Konfetti	confetti
der geschmückte Plattformwagen	decorated float
der Tanz, der Tanzabend	dance
die Taufe	christening, baptism
der Tod	death
der Zirkus	circus

seinen Geburtstag **feiern** to celebrate one's birthday
der Silvestertanz New Year's Eve dance
jemandem ein Geschenk machen to give somebody
 a present
Feuerwerk abbrennen to set off fireworks
ihr dritte Hochzeitstag their second (wedding)
 anniversary
beglückwünschen (zu) to congratulate (on)
wünschen to wish
(herzlich) Willkommen! you are (very) welcome!
in Trauer in mourning

KALENDER—BESONDERE EREIGNISSE

die Blaskapelle	brass band
das Fest	fête; feast (day)
die Flitterwochen *(pl)*	honeymoon *(time)*
das Folksongfestival	folk music festival
die Geburt	birth
die Hochzeit	wedding
die Hochzeitsreise	honeymoon (*journey*)
der Jahrmarkt	fair
die Messe	(commercial) fair
der Namenstag	saint's day
das Neujahrsgeschenk	New Year's gift, Christmas box
der Ruhestand	retirement
der Rummelplatz	funfair
die Trauung, -en	wedding ceremony
die Verlobung	engagement
die Zeremonie	ceremony

auf eine *or* **zu einer Hochzeit gehen** to go to a wedding
silberne/goldene/diamantene Hochzeit silver/golden/diamond wedding
in den Ruhestand treten to retire, go into retirement
die Stadt mit Blumen ausschmücken to decorate the town with flowers
die ganze Stadt war beflaggt there were flags out all over town
gute Vorsätze fassen to make good resolutions
beerdigen to bury

G.W.—D

* KLEIDUNG *(m)*

der **Anorak**, -s	anorak
der **Anzug**, ⸚e	suit
der **Badeanzug**, ⸚e	swimsuit
der **Handschuh**, -e	glove
der **Hut**, ⸚e	hat
der **Mantel**, ⸚	coat, overcoat
der **Pullover**,	
der **Pulli**, -s	pullover, jumper, sweater, jersey
der **Pyjama**, -s	(pair of) pyjamas
der **Regenmantel**, ⸚	raincoat
der **Rock**, ⸚e	skirt
der **Schal**, -e *or* -s	scarf *(long)*
der **Schlafanzug**, ⸚e	(pair of) pyjamas
der **Schlips**, -e	tie
der **Schuh**, -e	shoe
der **(Spazier)stock**, ⸚e	cane, walking stick
der **Stiefel**	boot
der **Strumpf**, ⸚e	stocking, (long) sock

einen Hut tragen *or* **aufhaben** to wear a hat
Hosen/einen Mantel tragen *or* **anhaben** to wear trousers/a coat
sich **anziehen** to get dressed, put on one's clothes
sich **ausziehen** to get undressed, take off one's clothes
sich **umziehen** to get changed, change one's clothes
seinen Hut **aufsetzen** to put on one's hat
seine Hosen/seinen Mantel **anziehen** to put on one's trousers/one's coat
seinen Hut **abnehmen** to take off one's hat
seine Hosen/seinen Mantel **ausziehen** to take off one's trousers/one's coat

* KLEIDUNG (*f*)

die Badehose, -n	swimming trunks
die Bluse, -n	blouse
die Brille, -n	(pair of) glasses
die Handtasche, -n	handbag
die Hose, Hosen (*pl*)	(pair of) trousers
die Jacke, -n	jacket
die Kappe, -n	cap
die Kleidung (*sg*)	clothes
die Krawatte, -n	tie
die Mode, -n	fashion
die Mütze, -n	cap
die Socke, -n	sock
die Tasche*, -n	pocket; bag

in Mode in fashion
modisch fashionable
altmodisch old-fashioned
sehr schick very smart
das steht Ihnen (gut) that suits you

* KLEIDUNG *(nt)*

das Hemd, -en	shirt
das Jackett, -s *or* -e	jacket
das Kleid, -er	dress
die Kleider	clothes
das Kopftuch, ¨er	headscarf, square
das Taschentuch, ¨er	handkerchief
die (Blue)jeans *(pl)*	jeans

** KLEIDUNG *(m)*

der Büstenhalter,	
der BH	bra, brassiere
der Gürtel	belt
der Hausschuh, -e	slipper
die Hosenträger *(pl)*	braces
der Knopf, ¨e	button
der Kragen	collar
die Lumpen *(pl)*	rags
der Morgenrock, ¨e	dressing gown
der Regenschirm, -e	umbrella
der Reißverschluß,	
(-schlüsse)	zip
der Unterrock, ¨e	underskirt, petticoat

hemdsärmelig, in Hemdsärmeln in (one's) shirt
  sleeves
der Kleiderbügel coat hanger
die Kleiderbürste clothes brush
der Kleiderschrank wardrobe

sich verkleiden to disguise oneself
maskiert masked

** KLEIDUNG (f)

die Größe*, -n	size
die Lederhose, -n	(pair of) leather shorts
die Melone*, -n	bowler hat
die Sandale, -n	sandal
die Schürze, -n	apron
die Strumpfhose, -n	(pair of) tights
die Uniform, -en	uniform
die Unterhose, -n	(under)pants
die Wäsche*, -n	washing; (under)clothes, underwear

** KLEIDUNG *(nt)*

das Abendkleid, -er	evening dress (*for woman*)
das Brautkleid, -er	wedding dress
das Nachthemd, -en	nightdress
das T-Shirt, -s	T-shirt, tee-shirt
das Unterhemd, -en	vest
die Shorts *(pl)*	shorts

*** KLEIDUNG *(m)*

der Arbeitsanzug *(sg)*	dungarees
der Ärmel	sleeve
der Blouson, -s	bomber jacket
der Dufflecoat, -s	duffel coat
der Gesellschafts-anzug	evening dress (*for man*)
der Hosenanzug, ⸚e	trouser suit
der Overall *(sg)*	overalls
der Pfennigabsatz, ⸚e	stiletto heel
der Rollkragen	polo collar
der Schnürsenkel	shoelace
der Smoking, -s	dinner jacket
der Trainingsanzug, ⸚e.	tracksuit

maßgeschneidert, nach Maß angefertigt made to measure

Kleider von der Stange off-the-peg clothes, ready-to-wear clothes

etwas von der Stange kaufen to buy something off the peg

sich Maß nehmen (zu) to measure oneself (for), take one's measurements (for)

*** KLEIDUNG (f)

die Falte*, -n	pleat
die Fliege*, -n	bow tie
die Freizeitkleidung (sg)	casual clothes
die Plateausohlen (pl)	platform soles
die Schultertasche, -n	shoulder bag
die Strickjacke, -n	cardigan
die Tracht, -en	costume, dress (local, national)
die Unterwäsche (sg)	underclothes
die Weste, -n	waistcoat

*** KLEIDUNG (nt)

das Band*, ⸚er	ribbon
das Blouson, -s	bomber jacket
das Knopfloch, ⸚er	buttonhole
das Zubehör (sg)	accessories

im Nationalkostüm, in Nationaltracht in national costume or dress

hochhackig high-heeled; **flach** flat

eine Blume im Knopfloch tragen to wear a buttonhole

* KÖRPERTEILE (m)

der Arm, -e	arm
der Finger	finger
der Fuß, ̈e	foot
der Hals, ̈e	neck; throat
der Kopf, ̈e	head
der Körper	body
der Magen, - or ̈	stomach
der Mund, ̈er	mouth
der Rücken	back
der Zahn, ̈e	tooth

* KÖRPERTEILE (f)

die Hand, ̈e	hand
die Haut, Häute	skin
die Lippe, -n	lip
die Nase, -n	nose
die Seite*, -n	side
die Stimme, -n	voice
die Wange, -n	cheek

* KÖRPERTEILE (nt)

das Auge, -n	eye
das Bein, -e	leg
das Blut	blood
das Gesicht, -er	face
das Haar, die Haare (pl)	hair
das Herz, -en	heart
das Kinn, -e	chin
das Ohr, -en	ear

sich den Arm/das Bein brechen to break one's arm/
  leg
zu Fuß on foot
ein Tritt (*m*) a kick; a step
barfuß gehen to go *or* walk barefoot
auf Zehenspitzen gehen to go *or* walk on tiptoe
von Kopf bis Fuß from head to foot
den Kopf schütteln to shake one's head
mit dem Kopf nicken to nod one's head
sich (*dat*) **die Hand geben, sich** (*dat*) **die Hand
  schütteln** to shake hands
(mit der Hand) winken to wave (one's hand)
**jemandem ein Zeichen geben, jemanden herbei-
  winken** to beckon to somebody
auf etwas zeigen to point to something
glatte/rauhe Haut smooth/rough skin
naß bis auf die Haut soaked to the skin
sich die Nase putzen to blow one's nose
Nasenbluten haben to have a nose-bleed
die linke/rechte Körperseite the lefthand/righthand
  side of the body
neben mir at my side
eine leise/laute Stimme haben to have a low/loud
  voice
leise/laut sprechen to speak softly/loudly
mit leiser/lauter Stimme sprechen to speak in a
  low/loud voice
jemanden aus den Augen verlieren to lose sight of
  somebody
im Handumdrehen in the twinkling of an eye
etwas (kurz) ansehen to glance at something
sich (*dat*) **die Haare schneiden lassen** to have one's
  hair cut
sein Herz klopfte his heart was beating
das Doppelkinn double chin

** KÖRPERTEILE (m)

der Ell(en)bogen	elbow
der Knochen	bone
der Muskel, -n	muscle
der Nagel, ::	nail

** KÖRPERTEILE (f)

die Brust, ::e	breast; chest
die Ferse, -n	heel
die Figur, -en	figure
die Form, -en	figure
die Gestalt, -en	figure
die Kehle, -n	throat
die Körperform, -en	figure
die Schulter, -n	shoulder
die Stirn, -en	forehead
die Taille, -n	waist
die Zehe, -n	toe
die Zunge, -n	tongue

** KÖRPERTEILE (nt)

das Gehirn, -e	brain
das Handgelenk, -e	wrist
das Knie, -n	knee

sich (dat) **die Nägel schneiden/feilen** to cut/file one's nails

jemandem auf die Schulter klopfen to tap somebody on the shoulder

mit den Achseln or **Schultern zucken** to shrug one's shoulders

die Stirn runzeln to frown

auf den Knien on one's knees

kniend kneeling; **(nieder)knien** to kneel (down)

bis zum Knie im Wasser gehen to walk in water up to one's knees

sich den Knöchel verstauchen to sprain one's ankle

das geht mir auf die Nerven! that gets on my nerves!

biegen to bend; **strecken** to stretch

ein Puff (m) a knock; **ein Boxhieb** (m) a punch

*** KÖRPERTEILE (m)

der Brustkorb, ⸚e	chest
der Daumen	thumb
der Fußknöchel	ankle
der Kiefer	jaw
der Knöchel	ankle
der Nacken	nape of the neck
der Nerv, -en	nerve
der Schenkel	thigh
der Zeigefinger	forefinger

*** KÖRPERTEILE (f)

die Ader, -n	vein, artery
die Arterie, -n	artery
die Augenbraue, -n	eyebrow
die Augenwimper, -n	eyelash
die Büste, -n	bust
die Faust, Fäuste	fist
die Fußsohle, -n	sole of the foot
die Hüfte, -n	hip
die Leber, -n	liver
die Lunge, -n	lung
die Niere, -n	kidney
die Pupille, -n	pupil (of eye)
die Rippe, -n	rib
die Schläfe, -n	temple
die Schlagader, -n	artery
die Wade, -n	calf (of leg)

*** KÖRPERTEILE (nt)

das Augenlid, -er	eyelid
das Blutgefäß, -e	blood vessel
das Fleisch	flesh
das Gelenk, -e	joint
das Genick, -e	nape of the neck
das Glied, -er	limb
das Rückgrat, -e	spine, backbone
das Skelett, -e	skeleton

* AUF DEM LANDE (m)

der Acker, ⸚	field
der Bach, ⸚e	stream, brook
der Bauer, -n	farmer, countryman
die Bauern (pl)	countryfolk, country people
der Bauernhof, ⸚e	farm
der Baum, Bäume	tree
der Berg*, -e	hill, mountain
der Bewohner	inhabitant
der Boden*, ⸚	soil, ground, earth
der Einwohner	inhabitant
der Erdboden, ⸚	soil, ground, earth
der Fluß, Flüsse	river, stream
der Friede(n)	peace
der Grund*	ground, soil
der Gummistiefel	wellington (boot)
der Hügel	hill
der Kreis*, -e	district
der Landstrich, -e	district
der Landwirt, -e	farmer
der Lärm	noise
der Laut, -e	sound
der Pfad, -e	path
der Schlamm, -e	mud
der See, -n	lake
der Spazierstock, ⸚e	cane, (walking) stick
der Stecken	stick
der Stein, -e	stone, rock
der Stiefel	boot
der Stock, ⸚e	cane; stick
der Strom, ⸚e	river
der Turm, ⸚e	tower
der Wald, ⸚er	wood, forest
der Weg*, -e	path, way, road

auf dem Lande in the country
aufs Land to the country
im Freien, unter freiem Himmel in the open air
Ferien auf dem Bauernhof farm holidays

* AUF DEM LANDE (*f*)

die **Bäuerin**	peasant (woman); farmer's wife
die **Bauersfrau, -en**	country woman, peasant (woman)
die **Brücke*, -n**	bridge
die **Burg, -en**	castle
die **Butterblume, -n**	buttercup
die **Erde, -n**	soil, ground, earth
die **Gegend, -en**	district
die **Hecke, -n**	hedge
die **Höhle, -n**	cave, den
die **Landbevölkerung** (*sg*)	countryfolk, country people
die **Landschaft**	countryside, landscape, scenery
die **Landstraße, -n**	(high) road
die **Luft**	air
die **Mühle, -n**	mill
die **Straße*, -n**	road
die **Windmühle, -n**	windmill

* AUF DEM LANDE (*nt*)

das **Bauernhaus, (-häuser)**	farmhouse
das **Blatt, ̈er**	leaf
das **Dorf, ̈er**	village
das **Feld, -er**	field
das **Gebiet, -e**	district
das **Geräusch, -e**	noise
das **Heu**	hay
das **Land*, ̈er**	country; countryside
das **Loch, ̈er**	hole
das **Schloß*, ̈sser**	castle
das **Tor*, -e**	gate

fruchtbar fertile, rich, productive
unfruchtbar infertile, poor, unproductive

** AUF DEM LANDE (m)

der Bezirk, -e	district
der Busch, ¨e	bush
der Forst, -e	forest
der Gasthof, ¨e	inn
der Gipfel	(mountain) top
der Graben, ¨	ditch
der Grundbesitz	property, estate
der Matsch	mud
der Staub	dust
der Wasserfall, ¨e	waterfall
der Wegweiser	signpost
der Weiler	hamlet
der Wipfel	tree-top

** AUF DEM LANDE (f)

die Ebene, -n	plain
die Ernte, -n	harvest, crop
die Feldfrucht, ¨e	crop
die Jagd	hunt; hunting; shooting
die Jugendherberge, -n	youth hostel
die Quelle, -n	spring, source
die Spitze*, -n	top, peak, point

** AUF DEM LANDE (nt)

das Fernglas (sg)	(pair of) binoculars
das Flachland, ¨er	plain
das Gasthaus, (-häuser)	inn
das Getreide	corn
das Grundstück, -e	property
das Gut, ¨er	estate
das Jagen	hunting; shooting
das kleine Dorf, -n ¨er	hamlet
das kleine Wohnhaus, -n -häuser	cottage
das Korn	corn
das Schießen	shooting
das Tal, ¨er	valley
das Ufer	bank (of river)
das Wirtshaus, ¨er	inn

*** AUF DEM LANDE (m)

der (Ab)hang, ∷e	slope
der Mast*, -e(n)	pylon
der Steinbruch, ∷e	quarry
der Sumpf, ∷e	marsh
der Teich, -e	pond
der Verwaltungs-bezirk, -e	administrative district
der Weiher	pond, small lake

*** AUF DEM LANDE (f)

die Besitzung, -en	estate
die Erika	heather
die Falle, -n	trap
die Gemeinde, -n	community
die Heide, -n	heather; heath
die Ruinen (pl)	ruins
die Wiese, -n	meadow

*** AUF DEM LANDE (nt)

das Heidekraut	heather
das Heideland	heath
das Heidemoor, -e,	moor
das Hochmoor, -e	moor
das Schilf, -e,	reed
das (Schilf)rohr, -e	reed
die Trümmer (pl)	ruins

in einer Jugendherberge übernachten to spend the
  night in a youth hostel
auf die Jagd gehen, jagen to go hunting or shooting
die Ernte einbringen to bring in the harvest
zur Erntezeit at harvest time
in der Ferne in the distance; in der Nähe nearby
sich auf den Weg machen to set out, set off
auf dem Rückweg, auf der Rückfahrt on the way
  back
sich verirren to get lost, lose one's way
wir gingen or stiegen den Berg hinauf we climbed
  (up) the hill

LÄNDER DER WELT

All countries are neuter unless marked otherwise. Where an article is shown, the noun is used with the article.

Afrika	Africa
Asien	Asia
Australien	Australia
Belgien	Belgium
Brasilien	Brazil
Bulgarien	Bulgaria
China	China
Dänemark	Denmark
Deutschland	Germany
England	England
Europa	Europe
Finnland	Finland
Frankreich	France
Großbritannien	Great Britain
Griechenland	Greece
Holland	Holland
Indien	India
Irland	Ireland
Italien	Italy
Japan	Japan
Jugoslawien	Yugoslavia
Kanada	Canada
Korea	Korea
Luxemburg	Luxemburg
Marokko	Morocco
Mexiko	Mexico
Neuseeland	New Zealand
die Niederlande (pl)	the Netherlands
Norwegen	Norway
Österreich	Austria
Pakistan	Pakistan
Polen	Poland
Portugal	Portugal
Rumänien	Rumania
Rußland	Russia

LÄNDER DER WELT

Schottland	Scotland
Schweden	Sweden
die **Schweiz**	Switzerland
Skandinavien	Scandinavia
die **Sowjetunion**	the Soviet Union, Russia
Spanien	Spain
Südafrika	South Africa
Südamerika	South America
die **Tschechoslowakei**	Czechoslovakia
die **Türkei**	Turkey
die **UdSSR**	USSR, Russia
die **Vereinigten Staaten**	the United States (of
(*mpl*) (**von Amerika**)	America)
Vietnam	Vietnam
Wales	Wales

in die **Niederlande/in die Sowjetunion fahren** to go
   to the Netherlands/to the Soviet Union
nach Deutschland/Österreich fahren to go to
   Germany/Austria
ins Ausland fahren *or* **gehen** to go *or* travel abroad
im Ausland sein to be abroad
von Übersee from overseas
ein Ausländer a foreigner
ein Fremder a stranger
ausländisch foreign
fremd strange, foreign
der **gemeinsame Markt** the Common Market

* MATERIALIEN (m)

der Bindfaden, :	string
der Draht, :e	wire
der Faden, :	thread
der Karton, -s	cardboard; cardboard box
der Pelz, -e	fur
der Samt	velvet
der Satin	satin
der Stein, -e	stone, rock
der Stoff, -e	cloth; material

* MATERIALIEN (f)

die Baumwolle	cotton
die Pappe	cardboard
die Plastik	plastic
die Schnur*, :e	string
die Seide	silk
die Wolle	wool

* MATERIALIEN (nt)

das Benzin	petrol
das Gas	gas
das Glas*	glass
das Gold	gold
das Holz	wood
das Leder	leather
das Material, -ien	material, cloth; material(s)
das Metall, -e	metal
das Nylon	nylon
das Öl	oil
das Papier	paper
das Plastik	plastic
das Seil	rope; cable
das Silber	silver

ein Pelzmantel (m) a fur coat
ein Lammfellmantel a sheepskin coat
eine Baumwollbluse a cotton blouse
ein Pappkarton (m) a cardboard box
ein Seidenschal (m) a silk scarf
ein Wollpullover (m) a woollen jumper
ein Holzstuhl (m) a wooden chair
die Tasche ist aus Leder the bag is made of leather
die Vase ist aus Ton the vase is made of earthenware
eisern iron
golden gold, golden
hölzern wooden
silbern silver

** MATERIALIEN (m)

der Backstein, -e	brick
der Cord	cord, corduroy
der Stahl	steel
der Ziegelstein, -e	brick

** MATERIALIEN (f)

die Bronze	bronze
die Kohle	coal
die Leinwand	linen; canvas
die Spitze*	lace (in *compounds*)
die Strickwaren (pl)	knitwear

** MATERIALIEN (nt)

das Eisen	iron
das Leinen	linen
das Porzellan	porcelain, china
das Schaffell	sheepskin
das Stroh	straw

*** MATERIALIEN (m)

der Beton	concrete
der Denim	denim
der Granit	granite
der Jeansstoff	denim
der Kalk	lime
der Kautschuk	(india)rubber (*substance*)
der Klebstoff	glue
der Kristall	crystal
der Marmor	marble
der Polyester	polyester
der Ton*	clay
der Tweed	tweed
der Zement	cement

*** MATERIALIEN (f)

die Flüssigkeit	liquid
die Töpferwaren (*pl*)	pottery

*** MATERIALIEN (nt)

das Baumwollgewebe	cotton fabric
das Blech	tin
das Blei	lead
das Fell, –e	fur, pelt
das Hartzinn	pewter
das Kupfer	copper
das Messing	brass
das Petroleum	paraffin
das Segeltuch	sailcloth, canvas
das Steingut	earthenware
das Wachs	wax
das Wildleder	suede
das wollene Tuch,	
das Wollzeug	woollen cloth
das Zinn	pewter

* AM MEER (m)

der Anker	anchor
der Ausflug, ¨e	trip, outing
der Badeanzug, ¨e	swimming *or* bathing costume, swimsuit
Badende(r), -n	bather
der Fahrgast, ¨e	passenger
der Fahrpreis, -e	fare
der Hafen, ¨	port, harbour
der Kahn, ¨e	boat
der Leuchtturm, ¨e	lighthouse
der Matrose, -n	sailor
der Passagier, -e	passenger
Reisende(r), -n	passenger
der Sand	sand
der Schwimmer	swimmer
der Seehafen, ¨	port
der Seemann, (-leute),	
der Segler	sailor
der Spaziergang, ¨e	walk
der Stein, -e	stone, rock
der Strand, ¨e	shore, beach
der Urlauber	holiday-maker

ans Meer *or* an die See fahren to go to the seaside
ertrinken to drown, be drowned
ertränken to drown (*someone or something*)
sinken to sink (*of boat*)
anlegen to moor (*of boat*)
untergehen to sink, go under
tauchen to dive; retten to save
spritzen to splash; waten to wade, paddle
seekrank werden to be *or* become seasick

* AM MEER (f)

die Badehose, -n	swimming or bathing trunks
die Badende, -n	bather
die Gezeiten (pl)	tide
die Insel, -n	island
die Küste, -n	coast, shore
die Reisende, -n	passenger
die Schwimmerin	swimmer
die See, -n	sea
die Seglerin	sailor
die Spritztour, -en	trip
die Strömung, -en	current
die Urlauberin	holiday-maker
die Welle, -n, die Woge, -n	wave

* AM MEER (nt)

das Bad*, ̈er	bathe (in sea)
das Boot, -e	small boat
das Fahrgeld, -er	fare
das Meer, -e	ocean, sea
das Picknick, -e or -s	picnic
das Schiff, -e	ship, vessel
das Schwimmen	swimming
das Ufer*	shore (lake); bank (river)
das Wasser	water

ruhig calm; **stürmisch** stormy; **rauh** rough; **bewegt** choppy

vom Winde getrieben werden to drift, be carried along by the wind

am Meer at the seaside; **auf offenem Meer, auf offener See** out at sea, on the open sea

auf dem/den (Meeres)grund at/to the bottom of the sea

es ist Flut/Ebbe the tide is in/out

schwimmen gehen, zum Schwimmen gehen to go for a swim

an or **auf Deck gehen** to go on deck; **auf Deck sein** to be on deck

** AM MEER (m)

der Bikini, -s	bikini
der Fischer	fisherman
der Horizont, -e	horizon
Insasse(r), -n	passenger
der Jachthafen, ̈	marina
der Ozean, -e	ocean
der Rettungsring, -e	lifebelt
der Rettungs-	
schwimmer	lifeguard
der Riemen	oar
der Sonnenstich	sunstroke
der Yachthafen, ̈	marina

** AM MEER (f)

die Besatzung, -en	crew
die Bucht, -en	bay
die Ebbe, -n	low tide
die Fahne, -n	flag
die Fähre, -n	ferry(-boat)
die Flagge, -n	flag
die Flotte, -n	navy, fleet
die Flut, -en	high tide
die Klippe, -n	cliff
die Last, -en	load, cargo
die Luftmatratze, -n	li-lo, air-bed
die Mannschaft, -en	crew
die Muschel(schale),	
-n and (-n)	shell
die Sandburg, -en	sandcastle
die Schwimmweste, -n	life jacket
die Sonnenbrille, -n	(pair of) sunglasses
die Überfahrt, -en	crossing

** AM MEER (nt)

das Deck, -s or -e	deck (of ship)
das Fischerboot, -e	fishing boat
das Ruder*	oar; rudder
das Segel	sail
das Teleskop	telescope

*** AM MEER (m)

der Badewärter	lifeguard
der Brückenpfeiler	pier
der Hafendamm, ̈e	pier; jetty
der Kai, -e *or* -s	quay, quayside, pier
der Kiesel(stein), - *and* (-e)	pebble
der Landungssteg, -e	jetty
der Liegestuhl, ̈e	deckchair
der Mast*(baum), -e(n) *and* (-bäume)	mast
der Pfeiler, der Pier	pier
der Schaum	foam
der Schiffbruch	shipwreck
die Schiffbrüchigen (*pl*)	shipwrecked (people)
der Schornstein*, -e	funnel
der (See)tang, -e	seaweed

*** AM MEER (f)

die Gangway	gangway
die (Kommando)brücke, -n	bridge (*of ship*)
die Kreuzfahrt, -en	cruise
die (Meeres)alge, -n	seaweed
die Mole, -n	pier; jetty
die Möwe, -n	seagull
die Mündung, -en	mouth (*of river*)
die (Schiffs)fracht, -en, die (Schiffs)ladung, -en	cargo
die Schindel, -n	shingle
die Seeluft	sea air
die Vergnügungsfahrt, -en	pleasure cruise

*** AM MEER (nt)

das Floß, ̈e	raft
die Gewässer (*pl*)	waters
das (Schiffs)wrack, -s	(ship)wreck
das Seegras, ̈er	seaweed
das Steuer(ruder)	rudder

* MENSCH *(m)*

der Bart, ¨e	beard
der Herr, -en	gentleman
der Junge, -n	boy
der Mann*, ¨er	man
der Mensch, -en	human being; man, man-kind; fellow
der Schnurrbart, ¨e	moustache
der Zorn	anger

* MENSCH *(nt)*

das Alter*	age (of person)
das Aussehen	appearance
das Benehmen	behaviour; manners
das Gefühl, -e	feeling
das Haar, -e	hair
das Mädchen	girl

bärtig bearded; **glatt rasiert** clean-shaven
schnurrbärtig with a moustache
jung young; **alt** old; **mittleren Alters** middle-aged
wie alt sind Sie? how old are you?, what age are
  you?
ich bin 16 Jahre alt I am 16 (years old)
müde/zornig/komisch aussehen to look tired/angry/
  funny
seinem Aussehen nach to judge by his appearance
ein gut aussehender Mann a handsome or good-
  looking man
er hat falsche Zähne he has false teeth
er hat blonde/dunkle/schwarze/rote/graue Haare he
  has blond or fair/dark/black/red/grey hair
rothaarig red-haired
kahl bald (of head); **gefärbt** dyed
lockiges/welliges or **gewelltes/glattes Haar** curly/
  wavy/straight hair
sich benehmen to behave oneself
ich habe das Gefühl, daß ... I have a feeling that ...
jemandens Gefühle verletzen to hurt somebody's
  feelings

* MENSCH (*f*)

die Brille, -n	(pair of) glasses
die Dame, -n	lady
die Figur, -en	figure
die Frau*, -en	woman
die Freude	joy
die Gesichtsfarbe, -n	complexion
die Glatze, -n	bald head
die Größe*	height; size
die Häßlichkeit	ugliness
die Schönheit	beauty
die Träne, -n	tear

Kontaktlinsen/eine Brille tragen to wear contact
  lenses/glasses
getönte Gläser tinted lenses
sie hat eine gute/schlechte Figur she has a good/bad
  figure
weinen to cry, weep; lachen to laugh; lächeln to
  smile
vor Freude lachen/weinen to laugh/cry with joy
lachen über + *acc* to laugh at
ein großer/kleiner Mann a tall/short *or* small man
ein Mann von mittlerer Größe a man of medium
  height, a medium-sized man
sie ist 1 Meter 70 groß she is 1 metre 70 tall
in Tränen ausbrechen to burst into tears
den Tränen nahe on the verge of tears
Krokodilstränen (*pl*) crocodile tears
er hat eine Glatze he is bald
pick(e)lig pimply, spotty
er hat Sinn für Humor he has a sense of humour
er/sie hat keine Falten im Gesicht he/she has no
  wrinkles on his/her face
ihre Frisur steht ihr gut her hairstyle suits her
sie ist von zierlicher/schlanker/schwerer Gestalt
  she is of a slight/slender/heavy build
die Gewohnheit haben, etwas zu tun to be in the
  habit of doing something
wie es seine Gewohnheit war as was his custom

** MENSCH (*m*)

der Ausdruck, ¨e	expression
der Charakter	character
der Pickel	spot, pimple
der Pony, -s	fringe
der Riese, -n	giant
der Sinn (für)	sense (of)
der Teint, -e	complexion
der Zwerg, -e	dwarf

** MENSCH (*f*)

die Bewegung, -en	movement
die Dauerwelle, -n	perm
die Falte*, -n	wrinkle
die Frisur, -en	hairstyle
die Gestalt, -en	build
die Geste, -n	gesture
die Gewohnheit, -en	habit
die Körperform, -en	figure
die Laune, -n	mood, humour
die Narbe, -n	scar
die Natur, -en	nature
die Pustel, -n	spot, pimple
die Stimmung, -en	mood, frame of mind
die Wut	fury, rage

** MENSCH (*nt*)

das Doppelkinn	double chin
das (Lebe)wesen	being; creature
das Wesen	character, personality

sie ist immer guter/schlechter Laune *or* **Stimmung**
she is always in a good/bad mood *or* humour
(nicht) in der Laune *or* **in der Stimmung für etwas sein** (not) to be in the mood for something
sich ärgern to be angry; **ärgerlich werden** to get angry; **rot vor Wut** red with anger; **eine Wut haben** to be in a rage; **wütend** furious
er gerät leicht in Wut he goes into a rage easily *or* for the slightest thing

*** MENSCH (m)

der Faulenzer,	
der Faulpelz, -e	lazybones
der Gang*, ¨e	walk, gait
der Gesichtszug, ¨e	(facial) feature
der Schönheitsfleck, -e	beauty spot
der Schweiß	perspiration, sweat
der Taugenichts	good-for-nothing
der Zug*, ¨e	feature

*** MENSCH (f)

die Ähnlichkeit, -en (mit)	similarity (to)
die Ängstlichkeit	timidity
die Eigenschaft, -en	quality (of person)
die Faulenzerin	lazybones
die Runzel	wrinkle
die Schande	shame, disgrace
die Schlafmütze	sleepyhead (male or female)
die Schüchternheit	shyness
die Sommersprosse, -n	freckle

*** MENSCH (nt)

das Gewissen	conscience
das Grübchen	dimple

verschwitzt sweaty, soaked with sweat (person)
schweißig sweaty (hands etc)
er sieht wie sein Vater/seine Mutter aus he looks like his father/his mother
er ist seinem Vater/seiner Mutter ähnlich he resembles his father/his mother
das sieht ihm ähnlich that's just like him
die Stirn runzeln to frown
sich jemandes/einer Sache schämen to be ashamed of somebody/something
sich schämen, etwas zu tun to be ashamed to do something
schäme dich! you should be ashamed of yourself!
reines/schlechtes Gewissen clear/bad conscience

ähnlich (+ *dat*)	similar (to), like
ängstlich	timid, fearful
ärgerlich (**auf** + *acc*)	annoyed (with)
auffallend	striking
blaß	pale
blind	blind
böse	bad; evil
böse (**auf** + *acc*)	angry (with)
sei mir nicht böse	don't be angry with me
braun	tanned
bucklig	hunch-backed
dick	fat (*person*)
dumm	stupid
dünn	thin
durchschnittlich, Durchschnitts-	average
ehrlich	honest
eifersüchtig (**auf** + *acc*)	jealous (of)
einsam	lonely
eng	narrow
enttäuscht	disappointed
ernst	serious
frech (**zu** + *dat*)	cheeky (to)
freundlich (**zu** + *dat*)	friendly (to), kind (to)
froh, fröhlich	glad; merry
gebräunt	tanned
geduldig	patient
geschickt	skilful, clever
grausam	cruel
groß	tall; big
gutmütig	good-natured, good-tempered
häßlich	ugly
hell	fair (*skin*); light
hübsch	pretty
intelligent	intelligent
klein	small
klug	clever
komisch	funny
kräftig	strong
kurzsichtig/weitsichtig	short-sighted/long-sighted

lächerlich	ridiculous
lahm	lame
lang	long
liebenswürdig	amiable, kind
mager	skinny, thin, lean
mürrisch	sullen, surly; grumpy
mutig	brave
nachlässig	careless
nackt	bare, naked
neidisch (auf + acc)	jealous (of)
nett	neat; nice (zu to)
reizend	charming
rund	round
schlank	slender
schön	beautiful
schüchtern	shy
schwach	weak
seltsam	strange
sonderbar	peculiar
sonn(en)verbrannt	sunburned
sorgfältig	careful, painstaking
stark	strong
stolz (auf + acc)	proud (of)
streng	hard, harsh; strict
stumm (vor)	dumb (with)
taub	deaf
traurig	sad
unartig	naughty
ungeschickt	clumsy, awkward
unruhig	restless
vernünftig	sensible
verrückt	crazy, mad
verschieden	different
vorsichtig	careful, cautious
weise	wise
winzig	tiny
zart	delicate, tender
zerstreut	absent-minded
zornig	angry
zufrieden (mit)	pleased (with)

* MÖBEL (m)

der Eßtisch, -e	dining table
der (Farb)fernsehapparat, -e,	
der (Farb)fernseher	(colour) television set
der Fernsprecher	telephone
der Kleiderschrank, ::e	wardrobe
der Kühlschrank, ::e	fridge, refrigerator
der Lehnsessel,	
der Lehnstuhl, ::e	armchair
der Plattenspieler	record player
der Raum*, Räume	room
der Schrank, ::e	cupboard
der Schreibtisch, -e	writing desk
der Sessel	armchair
der Spiegel	mirror
der Stuhl, ::e	chair
der Teppich, -e	carpet, rug
der Tisch, -e	table
der Vorhang, ::e	curtain

ein Zimmer möblieren to furnish a room
ein möbliertes Zimmer a furnished room
eine Vierzimmerwohnung a four-room(ed) flat
ein Haus mit 4 Zimmern a 4-apartment house
bequem comfortable
unbequem uncomfortable
geräumig roomy
in dem Zimmer war es sehr eng it was very cramped
  in the room

* MÖBEL (f)

die Gardinen (pl)	curtains
die Lampe, -n	light, lamp
die Schublade, -n	drawer
die Uhr*, -en	clock

den Tisch (auf)decken/abräumen to lay or set/to clear the table

Vorhänge or Gardinen aufhängen to put up or hang curtains

die Vorhänge or Gardinen aufmachen or aufziehen/ zumachen or zuziehen to open/close the curtains, to draw the curtains (open or shut)

★ MÖBEL *(nt)*

das Bett, –en	bed
das Bild, –er	picture, painting
das Bord, –e	shelf
das (Farb)fernsehen	(colour) television
das Feuer	fire
das Haus, Häuser	house
die Möbel *(pl)*	furniture
das Möbel(stück)	piece of furniture
das Regal, –e	(set of) shelves
das Telefon, –e	telephone
das Zimmer	room

ins Bett gehen, zu Bett gehen to go to bed
das Bett machen to make the bed
(die) Betten machen to make the beds
im Fernsehen on television
das Feuer anzünden to light the fire
etwas anzünden to set fire to something
Feuer fangen to catch fire

** MÖBEL (m)

der Backofen, ⸚	oven
der Bücherschrank, ⸚e	bookcase
der Elektroherd, -e	electric cooker
der Gasherd, -e	gas cooker
der Herd, -e	cooker
der Hocker	stool
der Kassettenrecorder	cassette recorder
der Möbelwagen	removal van
der Sekretär, -e	bureau, writing desk

** MÖBEL (f)

die Anrichte, -n	sideboard
die Frisierkommode, -n	dressing table
die Geschirrspül- maschine, -n	dish-washing machine, dishwasher
die Kommode, -n	chest of drawers
die Kuckucksuhr -en	cuckoo clock
die Matratze, -n	mattress
die Nähmaschine, -n	sewing machine
die Schreibmaschine, -n	typewriter
die Standuhr, -en	grandfather clock
die Strickmaschine, -n	knitting machine
die Truhe, -n	chest, trunk
die Waschmaschine, -n	washing machine

, * MÖBEL *(nt)*

das (Bücher)regal, -e	bookcase, bookshelves
das Buchgestell, -e	(set of) bookshelves
das Gemälde	painting, picture
das Kinderbett(chen), -en *and* (-)	cot
das Klavier, -e	piano
das Rollo, -s,	
das Rouleau, -s	blind
das Schubfach, ¨er	drawer
das Sofa, -s	settee, couch
das Tonbandgerät, -e	tape recorder
das Transistorradio, -s	transistor (radio)

ein Zimmer ausräumen to clear out a room
ausziehen to move out
einräumen to move in, put in position (*furniture*)
einziehen to move in
umräumen to move about, rearrange (*furniture*)

*** MÖBEL (m)

der Couchtisch, -e	coffee table
die Kleiderhaken (pl)	coat hooks, coat rack
der Nachtstrom-(heiz)ofen, ¨	(night-)storage heater
der Nachttisch, -e	bedside table
der Rahmen	frame
der Satz*, (¨e) Tische	nest of tables
der Schaukelstuhl, ¨e	rocking chair
der Schirmständer	umbrella stand
der Schutzengel	baby's highchair
der Teewagen	trolley
der Teppichboden, ¨	fitted carpet, wall-to-wall carpet(ing)
der Umzug*, ¨e	removal

*** MÖBEL (f)

die Einrichtung	furnishings
die Stehlampe, -n	standard lamp
die Stereoanlage, -n	stereo unit
die Tiefkühltruhe, -n	freezer, deep freeze
die Wiege, -n	cradle

*, ** MUSIKINSTRUMENTE *(m)*

der **Dirigent, -en**	conductor *(of orchestra)*
der **Flügel***	grand piano
der **Jazz**	jazz
der **Leiter***	conductor *(of choir)*
der **Musiker**	musician
der **Ton***, **¨e**	note; key
der **Zuhörer**	listener
die **Zuhörer** *(pl)*	audience, listeners

*** MUSIKINSTRUMENTE *(m)*

der **Akkord**	chord
der **Dudelsack** *(sg)*	bagpipes
der **Kontrabaß, (-bässe)**	double bass
der **Solist, -en**	soloist
der **Taktstock**	conductor's baton
der **Triangel**	triangle

*, ** MUSIKINSTRUMENTE *(nt)*

das **Akkordeon, -s**	accordion
das **Becken** *(sg)*	cymbals
das **Klavier, -e**	piano
das **Konzert, -e**	concert; concerto
das **Musikinstrument, -e**	musical instrument
das **Opernhaus, (-häuser)**	opera house
das **Orchester**	orchestra; band

*** MUSIKINSTRUMENTE *(nt)*

das **Bügelhorn, ¨er**	bugle
das **Cello, -s or Celli**	cello
das **Fagott, -s or -e**	bassoon
das **Horn, ¨er**	(French) horn
das **Jagdhorn, ¨er**	bugle; hunting horn
das **Saxophon, -e**	saxophone
das **Streichorchester**	string orchestra
das **Tamburin, -e**	tambourine
das **Violoncello, -s or** (-celli)	violoncello
das **Waldhorn, ¨er**	(French) horn
das **Xylophon, -e**	xylophone

* MUSIKINSTRUMENTE *(f)*

die Flöte, -n	flute
die Geige, -n	violin, fiddle
die Gitarre, -n	guitar
die Kapelle, -n	band, orchestra
die Konzerthalle, -n	concert hall
die Musik	music
die Trompete, -n	trumpet
die Violine, -n	violin

** MUSIKINSTRUMENTE *(f)*

die Blockflöte, -n	recorder
die Harfe, -n	harp
die Musikerin	musician
die Note*, -n	note
die Oper, -n	opera; opera house
die Querflöte, -n	flute
die Saite, -n	string
die Taste, -n	(piano) key
die (große) Trommel	(big, bass) drum
die Ziehharmonika, -s	accordion

*** MUSIKINSTRUMENTE *(f)*

die Klarinette, -n	clarinet
die Mundharmonika	mouth organ, harmonica
die Musikkapelle, -n	band (*circus, military etc*)
die Oboe, -n	oboe
die Orgel, -n	organ
die Posaune, -n	trombone
die Solistin	soloist

Klavier/Gitarre spielen to play the piano/the guitar
Klavier üben to practise the piano
Musik hören to listen to music
der Musik zuhören to listen to the music
ins Konzert gehen to go to a concert
im Konzert at the concert
blasen to blow; **schlagen** to beat, strike
dirigieren to conduct

NATIONALITÄTEN (m)

ein **Afrikaner**	an African
ein **Amerikaner**	an American
ein **Araber**	an Arab
ein **Asiat**	an Asian
ein **Australier**	an Australian
ein **Belgier**	a Belgian
ein **Brasilianer**	a Brazilian
ein **Brite**	a Briton; (pl the British)
ein **Bulgare**	a Bulgar, a Bulgarian
ein **Chinese**	a Chinese
ein **Däne**	a Dane
Deutsche(r)	a German
ein **Engländer**	an Englishman
ein **Europäer**	a European
ein **Finne**	a Finn
ein **Franzose**	a Frenchman
ein **Grieche**	a Greek
ein **Holländer**	a Dutchman
ein **Inder**	an Indian
ein **Ire**	an Irishman
ein **Italiener**	an Italian
ein **Japaner**	a Japanese
ein **Jude**	a Jew
ein **Jugoslawe**	a Yugoslav
ein **Kanadier**	a Canadian
ein **Mexikaner**	a Mexican
ein **Neuseeländer**	a New-Zealander
ein **Norweger**	a Norwegian
ein **Österreicher**	an Austrian
ein **Pakistaner**	a Pakistani
ein **Pole**	a Pole
ein **Portugiese**	a Portuguese
ein **Rumäne**	a Rumanian
ein **Russe**	a Russian
ein **Schotte**	a Scotsman, a Scot
ein **Schwede**	a Swede
ein **Schweizer**	a Swiss
ein **Sowjetbürger**	a Soviet citizen
ein **Spanier**	a Spaniard

NATIONALITÄTEN (m) (Forts)

ein Tschechoslowake	a Czech, a Czechoslovakian
ein Türke	a Turk
ein Ungar	a Hungarian
ein Vietnamese	a Vietnamese
ein Waliser	a Welshman

The forms given above and on the following two pages are the noun forms. The corresponding adjectives begin with a small letter and end in -isch.

Most can be formed by changing -er(in) or -ier(in) to -isch. The main exceptions are as follows: **deutsch** (*German*), **englisch** (*English*), **französisch** (*French*), **schweizerisch** (*Swiss*), **sowjetisch** (*Russian*)

NATIONALITÄTEN (f)

eine Afrikanerin	an African (girl or woman)
eine Amerikanerin	an American (girl or woman)
eine Araberin	an Arab (girl or woman)
eine Asiatin	an Asian (girl or woman)
eine Australierin	an Australian (girl or woman)
eine Belgierin	a Belgian (girl or woman)
eine Brasilianerin	a Brazilian (girl or woman)
eine Britin	a Briton, a British girl or woman
eine Bulgarin	a Bulgarian (girl or woman)
eine Chinesin	a Chinese (girl or woman)
eine Dänin	a Dane, a Danish girl or woman
eine Deutsche	a German (girl or woman)
eine Engländerin	an Englishwoman, an English girl
eine Europäerin	a European (girl or woman)
eine Finnin	a Finn, a Finnish girl or woman
eine Französin	a Frenchwoman, a French girl
eine Griechin	a Greek, a Greek girl or woman
eine Holländerin	a Dutchwoman, a Dutch girl
eine Inderin	an Indian (girl or woman)
eine Irin	an Irishwoman, an Irish girl
eine Italienerin	an Italian (girl or woman)
eine Japanerin	a Japanese (girl or woman)
eine Jüdin	a Jewish girl or woman
eine Jugoslawin	a Yugoslav, a Yugoslavian girl or woman
eine Kanadierin	a Canadian (girl or woman)
eine Mexikanerin	a Mexican (girl or woman)
eine Neusee- länderin	a New-Zealander, a New Zealand girl or woman
eine Norwegerin	a Norwegian (girl or woman)
eine Österreicherin	an Austrian (girl or woman)
eine Pakistanerin	a Pakistani (girl or woman)

NATIONALITÄTEN *(f)*

eine Polin	a Pole, a Polish girl *or* woman
eine Portugiesin	a Portuguese (girl *or* woman)
eine Rumänin	a Rumanian (girl *or* woman)
eine Russin	a Russian (girl *or* woman)
eine Schottin	a Scotswoman, a Scots girl
eine Schwedin	a Swede, a Swedish girl *or* woman
eine Schweizerin	a Swiss girl *or* woman
eine Sowjet-bürgerin	a Soviet citizen
eine Spanierin	a Spaniard, a Spanish girl *or* woman
eine Tschechoslo-wakin	a Czech, a Czechoslovakian (girl *or* woman)
eine Türkin	a Turkish girl *or* woman
eine Ungarin	a Hungarian (girl *or* woman)
eine Vietnamesin	a Vietnamese (girl *or* woman)
eine Waliserin	a Welshwoman, a Welsh girl

* OBST UND OBSTBÄUME *(m)*
der Apfel, ¨ apple
der Apfelbaum, (-bäume) apple tree
der Obstbaum, (-bäume) fruit tree
der Obstgarten, ¨ orchard
der Pfirsich, -e peach

** OBST UND OBSTBÄUME *(m)*
der Birnenbaum, (-bäume) pear tree
der Pfirsichbaum, (-bäume) peach tree
der Wein*, -e vine
der Weinberg, -e vineyard
der Weinstock, ¨e vine

*** OBST UND OBSTBÄUME *(m)*
der Granatapfel, ¨ pomegranate
der Kern pip, stone (*in fruit*)
der Rhabarber rhubarb
der Walnußbaum,
(-bäume) walnut tree

* OBST UND OBSTBÄUME *(nt)*
das Obst fruit
das Stück Obst piece of fruit

blaue/grüne Trauben black/green grapes
reif ripe; unreif not ripe
reif werden, reifen to ripen
süß sweet; bitter sour, bitter
saftig juicy; trocken dry
hart hard; weich soft
faul, faulig rotten
Obst schälen to peel fruit
in einen Apfel beißen to bite an apple
Obst pflücken to pick fruit
Beeren sammeln to go berry-picking
die Feige, -n fig
Rosinen (*fpl*) raisins
Sultaninen (*fpl*) sultanas
Korinthen (*fpl*) currants

* OBST UND OBSTBÄUME (f)

die **Ananas**, - *or* -se	pineapple
die **Apfelsine**, -n	orange
die **Banane**, -n	banana; banana tree
die **Beere**, -n	berry
die **Birne**, -n	pear
die **Erdbeere**, -n	strawberry
die **Frucht**, ⁀e	(particular kind of) fruit
die **Himbeere**, -n	raspberry
die **Orange**, -n	orange; orange tree
die **Zitrone**, -n	lemon

** OBST UND OBSTBÄUME (f)

die **Aprikose**, -n	apricot; apricot tree
die **Erdnuß**, (-nüsse)	peanut
die **Grapefruit**	grapefruit
die **Kastanie**, -n	chestnut
die **Kirsche**, -n	cherry
die **Melone***, -n	melon
die **Nuß**, Nüsse	nut
die **Pampelmuse**, -n	grapefruit
die **Pflaume**, -n	plum
die **Schale**, -n	skin (*of fruit*)
die **Traubenbeere**, -n	grape
die **Traubenlese**	grape harvest, vintage
die **(Wein)rebe**, -n	vine
die **(Wein)traube**, -n	bunch of grapes
die **Zwetsche**, -n	plum

*** OBST UND OBSTBÄUME (f)

die **Backpflaume**, -n	prune
die **Brombeere**, -n	blackberry, bramble
die **Dattel(palme)**, -n *and* (-n)	date (palm)
die **Haselnuß**, (-nüsse)	hazelnut
die **Heidelbeere**, -n	bilberry
die **Johannisbeere**, -n	redcurrant
die **schwarze Johannisbeere**, -n -n	blackcurrant
die **Stachelbeere**, -n	gooseberry
die **Walnuß**, (-nüsse)	walnut

* AUF DEM POSTAMT (m)

der Anruf, -e	telephone call
der Brief, -e	letter
der Briefkasten	letterbox; postbox, pillar box
der Briefträger	postman
der Fernsprecher	telephone
der Großbuchstabe, -n	capital letter
der Name*, -n	name
der öffentliche Fernsprecher	callbox
Postbeamte(r), -n	counter clerk
der Postsack, ˸e	mailbag
der Schalter	counter
der Stempel	stamp, postmark
der (Telefon)hörer	receiver (*part of telephone*)
der Umschlag, ˸e	envelope

** AUF DEM POSTAMT (m)

der Absender	sender
der Adressat, -en,	
der Empfänger	addressee
der Kugelschreiber	ballpoint pen
der Luftpostbrief, -e	airmail letter
der Telefonist, -en	(telephone) operator

senden, schicken to send; erhalten to receive

nachsenden to forward; zurückschicken to send back; aufgeben to post

mit der Post, per Post by post; per Luftpost by airmail

6 Briefmarken zu 70 Pfennig, 6 Siebziger Marken 6 70-Pfennig stamps

ist Post für mich da? is there any mail for me?

war die Post schon da? has the post come yet?

Lieber Franz! Dear Frank; Liebe Gertrud! Dear Gertrude

Dein Hans Your son *or* brother *or* friend *etc*, Jack

Deine Maria Your daughter *or* sister *or* friend *etc*, Mary

* AUF DEM POSTAMT (f)

die Adresse, -n	address
die Ansichtskarte, -n	picture postcard
die Antwort, -en	reply
die Auskunft*, ¨e	information; directory inquiries
die Blockschrift, -en	block or capital letter
die Briefkarte, -n	letter card
die Briefmarke. -n	(postage) stamp
die Fernsprechzelle, -n	telephone booth or box
die Leerung, -en	collection (of mail)
die Luftpost	airmail
die Nummer, -n	number
die Post*, -en post,	mail, letters; post office
die Postanweisung, -en	postal order
die Postbeamtin,	counter clerk
die Postkarte, -n	postcard
die Telefonzelle, -n	callbox, telephone booth or box or kiosk

** AUF DEM POSTAMT (f)

die Absenderin	sender
die Empfängerin	addressee
die Leitung*, -en	telephone line
die Paketpost	parcel post
die Postbestellung, -en	delivery (of mail)
die Telefonistin	telephone operator
die (Telefon)zentrale, -n	telephone exchange (in firm etc)
die Unterschrift, -en	signature
die Zustellung, -en	delivery (of mail)

Sehr geehrte (Damen und) Herren! Dear Sir (or Madam)

Viele Grüße!, Mit freundlichem or **herzlichem Gruß!** Best wishes

Herzliche Grüße or **Herzlichst (Dein** or **Ihr) Yours affectionately**

Hochachtungsvoll Yours faithfully

Mit freundlichen Grüßen Yours sincerely

* AUF DEM POSTAMT *(nt)*

das **Briefchen**	note, short letter
das **Briefpapier**	writing paper
das **Fernsprechbuch**, ¨er	telephone directory, telephone book
das **Formular**, -e	form
das **kleine Paket**, -n -e	
das **Päckchen**	packet
das **Paket**, -e	parcel
das **Porto**	postage
das **Postamt**, ¨er	post office
das **Postauto**, -s	mail van
das **Postwertzeichen**	(postage) stamp
das **Telefon**, -e	telephone
das **Telefonbuch**, ¨er	telephone directory, telephone book
das **Telefongespräch**, -e	phone call
das **Telefonhäuschen**	telephone kiosk
das **Telegramm**, -e	telegram, wire

** AUF DEM POSTAMT *(nt)*

das **Einwickelpapier**	wrapping paper
das **Ferngespräch**, -e	trunk call
das **Fernmeldewesen**	telecommunications
das **Fern(melde)amt**, ¨er	telephone exchange (*large*)
das **Klingeln**	ringing tone
das **Packpapier**	brown paper, wrapping paper
das **Streifband**, ¨er	(postal) wrapper

ein Formular ausfüllen to fill in a form
in Blockschrift, in Großbuchstaben, in Druckschrift in block letters, in capital letters
jemanden anrufen, jemandem telefonieren to phone somebody, call somebody (on the phone), give somebody a ring
ein (Fern)gespräch anmelden to make a (long-distance) call

*** AUF DEM POSTAMT (m)
die Drähte (pl) wires
der Einschreibebrief, -e registered letter
der Teilnehmer subscriber
der Telegrammbote, -n telegraph boy
der Telegraphenmast, -e(n) telegraph pole

*** AUF DEM POSTAMT (f)
die Drucksache, -n printed matter
die Frankierung prepaid postage
die Postgebühr, -en postage
die Wählscheibe, -n dial

*** AUF DEM POSTAMT (nt)
das Branchen-
 verzeichnis (sg) the Yellow Pages
das Einschreiben registration
das Ortsgespräch, -e local call
das Schreiben official or business letter
das Siegel seal

den Hörer abnehmen to lift the receiver
das Amtszeichen the dialling tone
(die Nummer) wählen to dial (the number)
durchwählen to dial direct
das Telefon läutet the telephone rings
antworten to answer
wer ist am Apparat, bitte? hello, who's speaking?
hier ist . . . this is . . .
bleiben Sie am Apparat hold the line please
(einen Augenblick,) ich verbinde Sie just a minute,
 I'll put you through
die Leitung ist besetzt the line is engaged
das Telefon ist nicht in Ordnung the phone is
 out of order
Sie sind falsch verbunden you have the wrong
 number
danke für den Anruf thanks for ringing or calling
ich rufe Sie zurück I'll call you back
den Hörer auflegen to replace the receiver

* RECHT (m)

der Anwalt, ⸚e	lawyer
der Ausweis, -e	identity card
der Bericht, -e	report
der bewaffnete Raubüberfall	armed hold-up
der Brand, ⸚e	fire
der Dieb, -e	thief
der Eigentümer	owner
Gefangene(r), -n	prisoner
der Geheimagent, -en	secret agent
der Held, -en	hero
der Inhaber	owner; occupant
der Kerl, -e	fellow, chap
der Mord, -e	murder
der Mörder	murderer, killer
der Polizist, -en	policeman
der Prozeß, -sse	lawsuit
der Raub (sg)	robbery
der Räuber	bandit, robber; hijacker
der Raubüberfall, ⸚e	robbery
der Rechtsanwalt, ⸚e	lawyer
der Revolver	gun, revolver
der Richter	judge
der Schutzmann, (-männer or -leute)	policeman
der Spion, -e	spy
der Typ, -en	fellow, chap
der Verbrecher	criminal, gangster
der Versuch, -e	attempt
der Zeuge, -n	witness

Hilfe! help!; haltet den Dieb! stop thief!
Feuer! fire!; Hände hoch! hands up!
stehlen to steal; erschießen to shoot (dead)
töten, umbringen to kill
ermorden to murder, assassinate
auf jemanden schießen to shoot (at) somebody
einbrechen in (+ acc) to break into, burgle
eine Bank ausrauben to rob a bank

* RECHT (f)

die Anzeige, -n	report
die Auskunft*, ¨e	information
die Ausweiskarte	identity card
die Bande, -n	gang
die Bank*, -en	bank
die Börse, -n	purse
die Diebin	thief
die Eigentümerin	owner
die Flucht, ¨-en	escape
die Gang, -s	gang
die Gefahr, -en	danger
die Gefangene, -n	prisoner
die Gerechtigkeit	justice
die Heldin	heroine
die Inhaberin	owner
die Justiz	justice
die Mörderin	murderess
die Pflicht, -en	duty
die Pistole, -n	gun, pistol
die Polizei	police
die (Polizei)wache*, -n	police station
die Polizistin	policewoman, WPC
die (Rechts)anwältin	lawyer
die Schuld	guilt
die Spionin	spy
die Tapferkeit	bravery
die Tasche*, -n	bag
die Unschuld	innocence
die Untersuchung*, -en	inquiry
die Verbrecherin	criminal
die Verhaftung, -en	arrest
die Wache*, -n	security guard
die Zeugin	witness

die Polizei holen lassen to send for the police
ein Polizist in Zivil a plain-clothes policeman
verhaften to arrest; überwältigen to overpower
schuldig guilty; unschuldig innocent
verdächtig suspicious; suspected

* RECHT (nt)

das Feuer	fire
das Gefängnis, -se	prison, jail
das Geld	money
das Gericht, -e	law court
das Gesetz, -e	law
das Gold	gold
das Recht, -e	the law; right
das Silber	silver
das Urteil, -e	judgment, verdict; sentence
das Verbrechen	crime
das Zuchthaus, (-häuser)	(top-security) prison

** RECHT (nt)

das Entkommen	escape
das Ergreifen	capture
das Gesetz, -e	law
das Gewehr, -e	gun, weapon
das Heer, -e	army
das Kidnapping, -s	kidnapping
das Meisterwerk, -e	masterpiece
das Plakat*, -e	placard; poster
das Polizeipräsidium	police headquarters

ein Verbrechen begehen to commit a crime
vor Gericht kommen *or* gestellt werden to be sent for trial
einen Zeugen befragen to question a witness
er wurde zu 3 Jahren Gefängnis verurteilt he was given a 3-year prison sentence, he was sentenced to 3 years in jail
jemanden ins Gefängnis bringen to put somebody in prison, imprison somebody
aus dem Gefängnis entkommen to escape from prison
freilassen to set free
entlassen werden to be released
auf Bewährung entlassen to let out on parole

** RECHT *(m)*

der Anschlag, ¨e	placard
der Bandit, -en	bandit
der Berichterstatter	reporter
der Betrüger	swindler, cheat
der Beweis, -e	evidence, proof
der Detektiv, -e	detective
der Diebstahl, ¨e	burglary
der Einbrecher	burglar
der Einbruch(dieb- stahl), ¨e *and* (¨e)	burglary
der Entführer	hijacker
der Feind, -e	enemy
der Flüchtling, -e	fugitive; refugee
der Gangster, -s	gangster
der Gauner	crook
der Gefängniswärter	prison guard
der Geldbeutel	purse
der Goldbarren	gold bar
der Hijacker	hijacker
der Kerker	dungeon
der Reisescheck, -s	traveller's cheque
der Retter	rescuer
der Rowdy, -s *or* -ies	hooligan
der Scheck, -s	cheque
der Schuß, ¨sse	(gun)shot
Sicherheits- beamte(r), -n	security guard
der Strafzettel	ticket, (parking) fine
der Streit, -e	argument, dispute
der Taschendieb, -e	pickpocket
der Tod, -e	death
Tote(r), -n	dead man
der Überfall, ¨e	hijack; attack
der Verdacht	suspicion
der Wächter	guard, security guard
der Wachtmeister	constable
der Wärter	(prison) guard

** RECHT (f)

die Armee, -n	army
die Aussage, -n	statement
die Beschreibung, -en	description
die Beschwerde, -n	complaint
die Brieftasche, -n	wallet
die Demonstration, -en	demonstration
die Einbrecherin	burglar
die Entführung, -en	hijack; kidnapping, abduction
die Gefangenschaft	imprisonment
die Geldstrafe, -n	fine
die Haft	imprisonment
die Rauferei, -en	scuffle
die Regierung, -en	government
die Retterin	rescuer
die Rettung, -en	rescue
die Schlägerei, -en	fight, brawl
die Todesgefahr	deadly danger, danger of death
die Todesstrafe	death penalty
die Tote, -n	dead woman
die Verhandlung, -en	trial
die Verurteilung, -en	sentence
die Vorladung, -en	notice
die Waffe, -n	weapon
die Zelle, -n	cell

entführen, hijacken to hijack; to kidnap, abduct
(in die Luft) sprengen to blow up (building)
demonstrieren to demonstrate
retten to rescue; heil; gesund und munter safe and
sound
ein tödlicher Unfall a fatal accident
am helllichten Tage in broad daylight
Trunkenheit am Steuer drunk driving
nüchtern sober; betrunken drunk
er wurde wegen zu schnellen Fahrens bestraft he
was fined for speeding

*** RECHT (m)

der Feigling, -e	coward
der Gerichtshof, ⸚e	law court
der Polizeikommissar, -e	police inspector
der Polyp, -en	'cop'
der Privatdetektiv, -e	private detective
der Terrorist, -en	terrorist
Verdächtige(r), -n	suspect

*** RECHT (f)

die Droge, -n	drug
die Festnahme, -n	arrest
die Klage, -n	accusation, complaint
die Kurzmeldung, -en	news flash
die Leiche, -n	corpse
die (Polizei)razzia, (-razzien)	(police) raid
die Terroristin	terrorist
die Verdächtige, -n	suspect

*** RECHT (nt)

das Bargeld	cash, ready money
das Barrengold	bullion
das Handgemenge	scuffle
das Loch*, ⸚er	hovel
das Lösegeld, -er	ransom
das Rauschgift, -e	drug
das Todesurteil	death sentence
das Verfahren	trial

drohen (+ *dat*), bedrohen to threaten
bestechen to bribe
belohnen to reward; strafen to punish
gehorchen (+ *dat*) to obey
mutig *or* tapfer sein to be brave; feig(e) sein to
be a coward
Angst haben to be afraid
wagen to dare

* SCHULE UND ERZIEHUNG (m)

der Bleistift, -e	pencil
der Erfolg, -e	success
der Federhalter	(fountain) pen
der Fehler	error, mistake
der Feiertag, -e	holiday, day off
der Fernsehapparat, -e,	
der Fernseher	television
die Fortschritte (pl)	progress
der freie Tag, -n -e	holiday, day off
der Freund, -e	friend
der Füllfederhalter	fountain pen
der Gang*, ̈e	corridor
der Gesang	singing
der Gummi, -s	rubber
der Hochschüler	college student
der Hof, ̈e	playground
der Irrtum, ̈er	error
der Kamerad	pal
der Kugelschreiber	ballpoint pen
der Kuli, -s	biro, ballpoint pen
der Lehrer	(school)teacher
der Lehrkörper	staff
der Preis*, -e	prize
der Schreibtisch, -e	desk
der Schulanfang	beginning of term
der Schüler	schoolboy, pupil, student
der Schulfreund, -e	schoolfriend
der Schulhof, ̈e	playground
der Schulkamerad, -en	schoolfriend
der Siegerpreis, -e	prize
der Spielplatz, ̈e	playground
der Student, -en	student
der Studienrat, ̈e	teacher (at secondary school)
der Stundenplan, ̈e	timetable
der Test, -s or -e	test
der Unterricht	teaching, lessons; education; instruction
der Vortrag, (-träge)	lecture

* SCHULE UND ERZIEHUNG *(f)*

die Aktentasche, -n	briefcase
die Arithmetik	arithmetic
die Aufgabe, -n	task, exercise
die Berufsschule, -n	technical college
die Erdkunde	geography
die Erzählung, -en	story
die Erziehung	education, schooling
die Fachschule, -n	technical college
die Feder*, -n	pen
die Ferien *(pl)*	holidays
die Frage, -n	question
die Freundin	friend
die Füllfeder, -n	fountain pen
die Geographie	geography
die Gesamtschule, -n	comprehensive school
die Geschichte, -n	history; story
die Grundschule, -n	primary school
die Hausaufgabe, -n	homework, exercise
die Hausaufgaben *(pl)*	homework; lessons
die Hochschule, -n	university
die höhere Schule, -n -n	secondary school
die Holzarbeiten *(pl)*	woodwork
die Kameradin	pal
die Karte*, -n	map
die Klasse, -n	class
die Kreide	chalk
die Kunst	art
die Lehrerin	(school)teacher, schoolmistress
die Lektion, -en	lesson
die Lektüre	reading
die Mathe	maths
die Mathematik	mathematics
die Mittelschule, -n	secondary school
die Musik	music
die Note*, -n	mark
die Prüfung, -en	exam, examination, test
die Rechenkunst	arithmetic
die Regel, -n	rule
die Schularbeiten *(pl)*	homework

* SCHULE UND ERZIEHUNG (f) (Forts)

die Schulaufgabe, -n	exercise
die Schule, -n	school
die Schülerin	schoolgirl, pupil, student
die Schulfreundin,	
die Schulkameradin	schoolfriend
die Schultasche, -n	satchel
die Seite* -n	page
die Sommerferien (pl)	summer holidays
die Studentin	student
die Studienrätin	teacher (at secondary school)
die Stunde*, -n	lesson, period
die Tafel*, -n	blackboard
die Tinte	ink
die Universität, -en	university
die Volksschule, -n	primary school
die Vorlesung, -en	lecture
die Zeichenkunst	drawing (subject)
die Zeichnung, -en	drawing (piece of work)

lernen to learn; **wiederholen** to repeat; to revise
Fortschritte machen to make progress
den ersten Preis gewinnen to win first prize
im Unterricht sein to be in class
zu spät zum Unterricht kommen to be late for class
einen Vortrag halten (über + acc) to give a lecture (on)
Ferien haben, in Ferien sein to be on holiday
in die Ferien gehen or **fahren** to go on holiday
jemandem eine Frage stellen to ask somebody a question
eine Prüfung machen/bestehen/nicht bestehen to take or sit/pass/fail an exam
in die Schule gehen, zur Schule gehen to go to school
die Schule besuchen to attend school
von der Schule abgehen to leave school
an die Tafel schreiben to write on the blackboard

* SCHULE UND ERZIEHUNG (nt)

das Abitur	school-leaving certificate
das Buch, ⸚er	book
das Deutsch	German
das Englisch	English
das Ergebnis, -se	result (of exam)
das Examen, - or Examina	exam, examination
das Französisch	French
das Gelingen	success
das Gymnasium, Gymnasien	grammar school
das Heft, -e	book
das Klassenzimmer	classroom, schoolroom
das Labor, -e or -s,	
das Laboratorium, Laboratorien	laboratory
das Latein	Latin
das Lehren	teaching
das Lexikon, Lexika	dictionary
das Lineal, -e	ruler
das Notizbuch, ⸚er	jotter; notebook
das Papier	paper
das Pult, -e	desk
das Rechnen	arithmetic
das Resultat, -e	result
das Schreibheft, -e,	
das Schulheft, -e	exercise book
das Schulmädchen	schoolgirl
das Schulzimmer	schoolroom
das Singen	singing
das Spanisch	Spanish
das Sprachlabor	language laboratory
das Staubtuch, ⸚er	duster
die Studien (pl)	studies
das Studium	study; studies
das Tonbandgerät, -e	tape recorder
das Unterrichten	teaching
das Wörterbuch, ⸚er	dictionary
das Zeichnen	drawing (subject)

** SCHULE UND ERZIEHUNG (m)

der Aufsatz, ⸚e	composition, essay
der Aufsichtsschüler	prefect
der Bericht, -e	report
der Bücherwart	book monitor
der Buchstabe, -n	letter of alphabet
der Direktor	headmaster (*of secondary school*)
der Filzschreiber	felt-tip pen
der Kindergarten, ⸚	nursery school
der Mitschüler	classmate, schoolmate
der Ordner	prefect
der Rektor	headmaster (*of primary school*)
der Satz*, ⸚e	sentence
der Schlafsaal, (-säle)	dormitory
der Schreibwarenwart	stationery monitor
der Schulleiter	headmaster
der Vertrauensschüler	prefect
der Wortschatz, ⸚e	vocabulary

in Großbuchstaben in capital letters, in block letters

das Abitur machen to do *or* take one's school-leaving certificate (*or* A-Levels *or* Highers)

das Abitur ablegen to obtain one's school-leaving certificate *etc*

Deutsch/Englisch/Französisch *etc* **sprechen** to speak German/English/French *etc*

jemanden in Latein unterrichten, jemandem Latein lehren to teach somebody Latin

Latein geben *or* **erteilen** to teach Latin

** SCHULE UND ERZIEHUNG (*f*)

die Algebra	algebra
die Aufsichtsschülerin	prefect
die Biologie	biology
die Chemie	chemistry
die Direktorin	headmistress (*of secondary school*)
die Garderobe*, -n	cloakroom
die gemischte Schule	mixed school, co-ed
die Geometrie	geometry
die Grammatik	grammar
die Handarbeit	needlework
die Koedukations-schule, -n	mixed school, co-ed
die Mappe, -n	briefcase
die Methode, -n	method
die Mitschülerin	classmate, schoolmate
die moderne Fremd-sprache	modern language
die Näherei	needlework
die Naturkunde	nature study
die Naturgeschichte	natural history
die neueren Sprachen	modern languages
die Pädagogische Hochschule, (P.H.), -n -n	College of Education
die Pause*, -n	break, interval
die Physik	physics
die Reihe*, -n	row (*of seats etc*)
die Rektorin	headmistress (*of primary school*)
die Religion	religion
die Schulleiterin	headmistress
die Sprache, -n	language
die Strafe	punishment
die Turnhalle	gym, gymnasium
die Übersetzung, -en	translation
die Übung, -en	practice; exercise

(moderne) **Fremdsprachen lernen, die neueren Sprachen studieren** to study modern languages
zur Strafe as a punishment

*** SCHULE UND ERZIEHUNG (m)

Abwesende(r), -n	absentee
die Anwesenden (pl)	those present
der Bleistiftspitzer	pencil sharpener
der Drehbleistift, -e	propelling pencil
der Internatsschüler	boarder
der Klecks, -e	blot
der Prüfer	examiner
der Religionsunter-richt	religious instruction
der Speisesaal, (-säle)	dining hall
der Tagesschüler	day-boy
der Tintenklecks, -e	ink blot
der (unvorbereitete) Übersetzungstext, (-n) -e	(unseen) translation (from a foreign language)

*** SCHULE UND ERZIEHUNG (f)

die Abwesende, -n	absentee
die Dichtung	poetry
die Hauswirt-schaftslehre	home economics
die Handelshoch-schule	commercial college
die Internatsschülerin	boarder
die Kantine, -n	canteen
die Poesie	poetry
die Preisverleihung	prize-giving
die Rechenmaschine, -n,	calculator
die Rechentabelle, -n	calculator
die Rechtschreibung	spelling
die Strafarbeit, -en	punishment exercise
die Tagesschülerin	day-girl
die technische Hochschule, -n -n	technical college
die Übersetzung (in die Fremdsprache)	prose translation (into the foreign language)

auswendig (off) by heart
faul lazy; fleißig hard-working

** SCHULE UND ERZIEHUNG (nt)

das Bestehen	pass (in exam)
das Diktat,	
das Diktieren	dictation
das Diplom -e	diploma
das Durchkommen	pass (in exam)
das Essay	essay
das Fach, ¨er,	
das Fachgebiet, -e	(school) subject
das Halbjahr, -e	term
das Italienisch	Italian
das Quartal	term
das Schulfach, ¨er	school subject
das Schulzeugnis, -se	report
das Semester	term
das Trimester	term
das Turnen*	physical education, P.E.
das Vokabular	vocabulary
das Wörterverzeich-nis, -se	vocabulary
das Zeugnis, -se	report, certificate

*** SCHULE UND ERZIEHUNG (nt)

das Benehmen	behaviour, conduct
das Betragen	behaviour
das Griechisch	Greek
das Internat, -e	boarding school
das Konzept, -e	rough copy
das Löschpapier	blotting paper
das Nachsitzen	detention
das Russisch	Russian
das Studenten(wohn)-heim, -e	students' hall of residence

jemanden **nachsitzen lassen** to keep somebody in
die Schule **schwänzen** to skip school, play truant
schulfrei haben to have a holiday
verbessern to correct, improve; **korrigieren** to
   correct; **strafen** to punish

* SPEISEN UND MAHLZEITEN (m)

der Durst	thirst
der Fisch, -e	fish
der Hunger	hunger
der Kaffee	coffee
der Käse	cheese
der Keks, -e	biscuit
der Kuchen	cake
der Löffel	spoon
der Nachtisch, -e	dessert, sweet
der Pfeffer	pepper
der Salat, -e	salad
der Schinken	ham
der Tee	tea (*drink*)
der Teller	plate
der Wein*, -e	wine
der Zucker	sugar

(m) TABAK

der Aschenbecher	ashtray
der Tabak	tobacco

(f) TABAK

die Pfeife, -n	pipe
die Zigarette, -n	cigarette
die Zigarre, -n	cigar

(nt) TABAK

das Feuerzeug, -e	lighter
das Streichholz, ⸚er	match

essen to eat; **trinken** to drink; **schlucken** to swallow;
  schmecken to taste
schmeckt Ihnen der Wein? do you like the wine?
bitten um to ask for; **reichen** to pass, hand
schneiden to cut; **einschenken** to pour (*tea etc*)
vorbereiten to prepare; **kochen** to cook; **backen** to
  bake; **braten** to fry; **würzen** to season
um Feuer bitten to ask for a light
anzünden to light (up); **rauchen** to smoke

* SPEISEN UND MAHLZEITEN (f)

die Bestellung, -en	order
die Büchse, -n	tin, can
die Butter	butter
die Dose, -n	box; tin, can
die Flasche, -n	bottle
die Früchte (pl)	fruit
die Gabel, -n	fork
die Limonade, -n	lemonade
die Mahlzeit, -en	meal
die Milch	milk
die Nachspeise, -n	dessert, sweet
die Sahne	cream
die Sauce, -n	sauce
die Schale, -n	bowl
die Schokolade, -n	chocolate
die Schüssel, -n	bowl, dish
die Soße, -n	sauce
die Speise, -n	food
die Suppe, -n	soup
die Tasse, -n	cup
die Untertasse, -n	saucer
die Vorspeise, -n	hors d'œuvre, starter

ich esse gern Käse I like (eating) cheese
ich trinke gern Tee I like (drinking) tea
ich mag Käse/Tee nicht, ich mag keinen Käse/Tee
   I don't like cheese/tea
hungrig sein, Hunger haben to be hungry
durstig sein, Durst haben to be thirsty
ich sterbe vor Hunger I'm starving
eine Büchse or eine Dose Milch a tin of (evaporated)
   milk; **eine Dose Cola** a can of Coke
haben Sie schon gegessen? have you eaten yet?
was haben Sie zum Mittagessen gehabt? what did
   you have for lunch?
(das Geschirr) abwaschen, das Geschirr spülen
   to wash the dishes, do the washing-up
den Tisch (auf)decken/abräumen to lay or set/to
   clear the table

G.W.—F

* SPEISEN UND MAHLZEITEN (nt)

das Abendessen	tea; dinner; supper
das Bier, -e	beer
das Bonbon, -s	sweet, sweetie
das (Brat)hähnchen	(roast) chicken
das Brot, -e	bread; loaf
das Butterbrot, -e	piece of bread and butter
das Dessert, -s	dessert
das Ei, -er	egg
das Eis*	ice cream
das Essen	meal
das Fleisch	meat
das Frühstück, -e	breakfast
die Gemüse (pl)	vegetables
das Gericht, -e	dish, course
das Geschirr*, -e	dishes, crockery
das Glas*, ̈er	glass
das Hauptgericht, -e	main course
das Mehl, -e	flour
das Messer	knife
das Mittagessen	lunch; dinner
das Obst	fruit
das Stück (-e) Obst	piece of fruit
das Öl	oil
das Omelett, -s	omelette
die Pommes frites (pl)	chips
das Rindfleisch	beef
das Salz	salt
das Schwarzbrot	rye bread
das Steak, -s	steak
das Tischtuch, ̈er	tablecloth
das Wasser	water
das Würstchen	sausage (small)

ein hartes/weiches Ei a (hard/soft) boiled egg
das Rührei scrambled eggs
das Spiegelei fried egg
das Osterei Easter egg
Schinken und Ei bacon and eggs

** SPEISEN UND MAHLZEITEN (m)

der Appetit, -e	appetite
der Brandy	brandy
die Chips (pl)	crisps
der Dessertlöffel	dessert spoon
der Essig	vinegar
der Eßlöffel	tablespoon
der Fruchtsaft, ⁚e	fruit juice
der Geschmack, ⁚e	taste
der Honig	honey
der Joghurt, -s	yoghurt
der Kaffeefilter	coffee-maker
der Kartoffelbrei	mashed potatoes
der Kognak, -s	brandy
der Korken	cork
der Krug (⁚e) Wasser	jug of water
der Milchtopf, ⁚e	milk jug
der Pfannkuchen	pancake
der Rahm	cream
der Reis	rice
der Rindsbraten	roast beef
der Schinkenspeck, -e	bacon
der Schlagrahm	whipped cream
der Speck, -e	bacon
der Strohhalm, -e	(drinking) straw
der Teelöffel	teaspoon
der Toast, -s	toast
der Weinbrand	brandy
der Whisky, -s	whisky
der Zwieback	toast (in packets)

guten Appetit! have a nice meal!, enjoy your meal!
ein belegtes Brot a sandwich
ein Käse-/Marmeladenbrot a cheese/jam sandwich
Obstkuchen mit Sahne fruit tart with cream
alkoholisch alcoholic; **alkoholfrei** non-alcoholic

** SPEISEN UND MAHLZEITEN (f)

die Eisdiele, -n	ice cream parlour
die Kaffeekanne, -n	coffee pot
die Margarine	margarine
die Marmelade, -n	jam
die Meeresfrüchte (pl)	seafood, shellfish
die Orangen-	
marmelade, -n	marmalade
die Schlagsahne	whipped cream
die Semmel, -n	roll
die Teekanne, -n	teapot
die Thermosflasche,	
-n	flask
die Vanillesoße	custard
die Wurst, ¨e	sausage (large)

** SPEISEN UND MAHLZEITEN (nt)

das Brötchen	roll
das (Coca) Cola	'Coke', Coca Cola
das Geflügel	poultry
das Getränk, -e	drink
das Kalbfleisch	veal
das Kartoffelpüree	mashed potatoes
das Sandwich, -es	sandwich
das Schweinefleisch	pork
das Tablett, -e	tray

bedienen Sie sich!, nehmen Sie sich! help yourself!

*** SPEISEN UND MAHLZEITEN *(m)*

der Apfelsaft	apple juice
der Champagner	champagne
der Eintopf, ¨e	stew
der Eiswürfel	ice cube
der Hamburger	hamburger *(with bread)*
der Imbiß, -sse	snack
der Kakao, -s	cocoa
der Sekt, -e	champagne
der Senf, -e	mustard
der Wackelpeter	jelly
der Zitronensaft	lemon juice
der Zitronentee	lemon tea

*** SPEISEN UND MAHLZEITEN *(f)*

die (Braten)soße	gravy
die Frikadelle, -n	hamburger
die Konserven *(pl)*	preserved foods
die Krume, -n	crumb
die Kutteln *(pl)*	tripe
die Leber, -n	liver
die Muschel, -n	mussel
die Niere, -n	kidney
die Serviette, -n	napkin, serviette
die Zuckerschale, -n	sugarbowl

*** SPEISEN UND MAHLZEITEN *(nt)*

das Festmahl, -e	feast
das Korinthen- brötchen	bun
das Kotelett, -e	chop
das Lammfleisch	lamb
das Radlermaß	shandy
das Schnitzel	(veal) cutlet
das Tutti Frutti	trifle

* SPORT (m)

der Anfänger	beginner
der Ball, ⸚e	ball
der Basketball	basketball
der Campingplatz, ⸚e	camp-site
der Champion, -s	champion
der Fußball, ⸚e	football
der Gegner	opponent
der Kampf*, ⸚e	match
der Lauf, (Läufe)	running; run
der Meister	champion
der Netzball	netball
der Neuling, -e	beginner
der Platz*, ⸚e	ground
der Rennsport	racing
der Rollschuh, -e	(roller) skate
der Schi, -er	ski
der Schiedsrichter	(*football, rugby*) referee; (*tennis*) umpire
der Schläger	racket
der Schlittschuh, -e	(ice) skate
der Sieger	winner
der Ski, -er	ski
der Spieler	player
der Spielstand, ⸚e	score
der Sport, -e	game, sport
der Tennisplatz, ⸚e	tennis court
der Torwart, -e	(goal)keeper
der Trainer	trainer, coach (*male or female*)
Unparteiische(r), -n	umpire
der Volleyball	volleyball
der Wettkampf, ⸚e	match
der Zuschauer*	spectator

Fußball/Netzball/Tennis spielen to play football/ netball/tennis
Sport treiben to go in for sports
laufen to run; **springen** to jump
werfen to throw; **trainieren** to train

* SPORT (f)

die Anfängerin	beginner
die (Aschen)bahn, -en	track
die Chance*, -n	opening
die Fläche*, -n	ground
die Führung	lead; leadership
die Fußballelf, -en,	
die Fußballmann-schaft, -en-	football team
die Gegnerin	opponent
die Jugendherberge, -n	youth hostel
die Kampfbahn, -en	stadium
die Kugel	bowl
die Mannschaft, -en	team
die Möglichkeit*, -en	opening
die Partie	game, match
die Punktzahl, -en	(final) score
die Schlußrunde, -n	final
die Siegerin	winner
die Spielerin	player
die Spitze*, -n	lead, top
die Unparteiische, -n	umpire
die Versammlung, -en	meeting
die Zuschauerin	spectator

das Spiel or **die Partie gewinnen/verlieren** to win/lose the game or match; **schlagen** to beat
wie steht das Spiel? what is the score?
ein Tor schießen to score a goal
der Schiedsrichter gibt einen Strafstoß the referee awards a penalty
das Spiel ging unentschieden aus the match was drawn or was a draw
an der Tabellenspitze stehen to be at the top of the league
die Führung übernehmen to take the lead
eine Mannschaft unter der Führung von . . . a team under (the leadership of) . . .

★ SPORT (*nt*)

das **Angeln**	fishing
das **Billard** (*sg*)	billiards
das **Boule** (*sg*)	bowls
das **Bowling**	bowls; tenpin bowling
das **Camping**	camping
das **Endspiel, -e**	final
das **Ergebnis, -se**	result
das **Federballspiel**	badminton
das **Finale, -(s)**	final
das **Fischen**	fishing
das **Golf(spiel)**	golf
das **Hockey**	hockey
das **Kricket**	cricket
das **Laufen**	running
das **Match, -es**	match
das **Radfahren,**	
das **Radsport**	cycling
das **Rennen**	racing, race meeting
das **Rugby**	rugby
das **Schwimmbad, ̈er,**	
das **Schwimmbecken**	swimming pool
das **Schwimmen**	swimming
das **Skifahren,**	
das **Skilaufen**	skiing
das **Spiel★, -e**	play; game, match
das **Spielergebnis, -se**	(final) score
das **Sportfeld,**	
das **Stadion**	stadium
das **Team, -s**	team
das **Tennis**	tennis
das **Tor★, -e**	goal
das **Training**	training
das **Turnier, -e**	tournament
das **Zelt, -e**	tent
das **Zelten**	camping
das **Ziel, -e**	goal, aim; finish

Zelten gehen to go camping
ein Zelt aufschlagen to pitch a tent

★★ SPORT (m)

der (abgesteckte) Spielplatz, ¨e	court
der Bergsteiger	climber, mountaineer
der Fußballanhänger,	
der Fußballfan, -s	football supporter
der Reitsport	horse-riding
der Ringrichter	(boxing) referee
der Satz*, ¨e	set (tennis)
der Schlafsack, ¨e	sleeping bag
der Stoß, ¨e	kick; push, thrust
der Torpfosten	goal post
der Tritt*, -e	kick
der (Welt)rekord, -e	(world) record
der Wettbewerb, -e	competition
der Zielpfosten	winning post

★★ SPORT (f)

die Bowlingbahn, -en	bowling alley
die Eisbahn, -en	ice rink
die Halbzeit	half (of match); half-time
die Meisterschaft, -en	championship
die Rennbahn, -en	race course, track
die Rennstrecke, -n	race track
die Spielhälfte, -n	half (of match)
die Tabellenspitze, -n	lead (in league etc)
die Zielstange, -n	winning post

★★ SPORT (nt)

das Bergsteigen	climbing, mountaineering
das Boxen	boxing
das Jagen	hunting; shooting
das Klettern	climbing, mountaineering
das Netz, -e	net
das Reiten	horse-riding
das Schießen	shooting
das Schlittschuhlaufen	skating
das Tischtennis	table tennis
das Turnen* (sg)	gymnastics
das Wettspiel, -e	tournament

*** SPORT (m)

der Anpfiff	kick-off; starting whistle
der Anstoß	kick-off
der Billardstock, ̈-e	billiard cue
der Einstand	deuce
der Golfplatz. ̈-e	golf course, links
der Golfschläger	golf club
der Hochsprung, ̈-e	high jump
der Kletterer	climber
der Paß*, ̈-sse	pass
der Pferderennsport	(horse-)racing
der Rodel(schlitten)	toboggan
der Rudersport	rowing
der Schlitten	sledge, toboggan
der Speer, -e	javelin
der Spurt, -s or -e	sudden spurt
der Titelverteidiger	(title-)holder
die Turnschuhe (pl)	gym shoes
der Vorkampf, ̈-e	heat
der Weitsprung, ̈-e	long jump
der Wintersport (sg)	winter sports
der Zeitnehmer	timekeeper
der Zwischenspurt, -s or -e	sudden spurt

wir gehen gern bergsteigen/skifahren/schlittschuh-laufen we like going mountaineering/skiing/skating
ich bin ein großer Pferdefreund I am a great horse-lover
Weitsprung/Hochsprung machen to do the long jump/the high jump
einen Wettbewerb/einen Wettkampf veranstalten to organize a competition/a match
die Olympischen Spiele finden alle vier Jahre statt the Olympic Games take place every four years
einen Rekord aufstellen to set a record
durch das Ziel laufen to pass the winning post

*** SPORT *(f)*

die (Ball)abgabe	pass
die Leichtathletik *(sg)*	athletics
die Mark*	touch
die Regatta, -s	boat race
die Runde, -n	lap, round
die Stoppuhr, -en	stopwatch
die Titelverteidigerin	(title-)holder
die Torlatte, -n	cross-bar
die Tribüne*, -n	stand, grandstand
die Turnhalle, -n	gymnasium
die Verteidigung	defence
die Zuschauertribüne, -n	stand, grandstand

*** SPORT *(nt)*

das Bogenschießen	archery
das Fechten	fencing
das Gedränge	scrum
das gemischte Doppel *(sg)*	mixed doubles
das Hangsegeln	hang-gliding
das Herreneinzel	men's singles
das Pferderennen	race meeting
das Queue	billiard cue
das Ringen	wrestling
das Rudern	rowing
das Tauchen	diving
das Tauziehen	tug-of-war
das Untertauchen	diving
das Wasserschilaufen	water-skiing

* IN DER STADT (m)

der Bahnhof, ¨e	railway station
der Bürgermeister	mayor
der Bürgersteig, -e	pavement
der Dom, -e	cathedral
der Einwohner	inhabitant
der Fußgänger	pedestrian
der Fußgängerüber- weg, -e	pedestrian crossing
der Kinderwagen	pram
der Laden*, ¨	shop
der Markt, ¨e	market
der Markttag, -e	market day
der Park, -s	(public) park
der Parkplatz, ¨e	parking place; car park
der Pfad, -e	path
der Platz*, ¨e	square
der Polizist, -en	policeman
der Stadtrand (sg)	the outskirts
der Straßenübergang	pedestrian crossing
der Turm, ¨e	tower
der Verkehr	traffic
der Weg*, -e	way
der Wegweiser	roadsign
der (Zeitungs)kiosk, -e,	
der (Zeitungs)stand, ¨e	(newspaper) stall

** IN DER STADT (m)

der Bau, -ten	building
der Bezirk, -e	district
der Biergarten, ¨	beer garden
der Bürger	citizen
der Busbahnhof, ¨e	bus or coach station
der Festzug, ¨e	procession, pageant
der Marsch, ¨e	parade
der Passant, -en	passer-by
der Staatsbürger	citizen
der Umzug*, ¨e	parade
der Wolkenkratzer	skyscraper
der Zug*, ¨e	procession, parade

* IN DER STADT (f)

die Allee, -n	avenue
die Bevölkerung	population
die Brücke*, -n	bridge
die Burg, -en	castle
die Bürgermeisterin	mayoress
die Bushaltestelle, -n	bus stop
die Ecke, -n	corner, turning
die Einbahnstraße, -n	one-way street
die Fabrik, -en	factory, works
die Fahrbahn, -n	roadway
die Großstadt, ⸚e	city
die Haltestelle, -n	(bus or tram) stop
die Hauptstraße, -n	main road; main street
die Kirche, -n	church
die Klinik, -en	hospital, clinic
die Kreuzung, -en	crossroads
die Menge, -n	crowd
die Polizei	police
die Post*, -en	post office
die Schlange*, -n	queue
die Stadt, ⸚e	town; city
die Stadtmitte, -n	town centre; city centre
die Straße*, -n	street; road
die Tankstelle, -n	service station, garage
die Umgebung	the surroundings
die Untergrundbahn, -en	underground (railway)
die U-Bahn, -en	
die Verkehrsstockung, -en	traffic jam
die Vorstadt, ⸚e	suburb
die Wache*, -n	police station

in die Stadt gehen to go or walk into town
eine Stadtrundfahrt or -gang machen to go on a
  tour of the city
über die Straße gehen to cross the street
auf der anderen Seite der Straße on the other side
  of the street; über der Straße across the street
Wachtmeister! Constable!

* IN DER STADT (*nt*)

die Außengebiete (*pl*)	the outskirts
das Gedränge	crowd
das Geschäft*, -e	shop
das Heft, -e	book (*of tickets*)
das Hotel, -s	hotel
das Kaufhaus, (-häuser)	large shop, department store; warehouse
das Kino, -s	cinema
das Krankenhaus, ¨er	hospital
das Museum, Museen	museum
das Parkhaus, ¨er	(covered) car park
das Plakat* -e	poster, notice
das Postamt, ¨er	post office
die Randgebiete (*pl*)	the outskirts
das Rathaus, ¨er	town hall
das Restaurant, -s	restaurant
das Schloß* ¨sser	castle
das Stadtzentrum	city centre, town centre
das Straßenschild, -er	roadsign
das Taxi, -(s)	taxi
das Theater	theatre
das Tor*, -e	gate(way), arch
das Werk, -e	factory, works

** IN DER STADT (*f*)

die Fahrt*, -en	tour
die Feuerwehrwache, -n	fire station
die Gasse, -n	lane, alley, back street
die Kunstgalerie, -n	art gallery
die Polizeiwache, -n	police station
die Prozession, -en	procession
die Reise*, -n,	
die Rundreise, -n	tour
die Spitze*, -n	spire
die Statue, -n	statue
die Tour, -en	tour

*** IN DER STADT (m)
der Abwasserkanal, -kanäle	sewer
der Betrieb	bustle
der Doppeldecker	double decker (bus)
der Eindecker, der einstöckige Omnibus	single decker (bus)
der Friedhof, ⸚e	cemetery, graveyard
der Landkreis, -e	county (German)
der Pflasterstein, -e	paving stone
der Rad(fahr)weg, -e	cycle track
der Stadtbewohner,	town dweller
der Städter	
der Taxistand, ⸚e	taxi rank
der Wohnblock, -s	block of flats

*** IN DER STADT (f)
die Abwasserleitung, -en	sewer
die Leuchtreklame, -n	neon sign
die Meinungsumfrage, -n	opinion poll
die Sackgasse -n	dead end
die Sehenswürdig- keiten (pl)	the sights, places of interest
die Siedlung, -en	housing estate
die Sozialwohnung, -en	council house
die Straßenecke, -n	street corner
die Straßenlaterne, -n	street lamp
die Umgehungsstraße, -n	by-pass

, * IN DER STADT (nt)
das Denkmal, ⸚er	monument
das Gebäude	building
das geschäftige Treiben	bustle
das Kopfsteinpflaster (sg)	cobblestones
das Monument, -e	monument
das Parken	parking
das Stadtviertel	district
das Verkehrsamt, ⸚er,	
das Verkehrsbüro, -s	tourist information office
das Viertel	district

* THEATER (m)

der Abgang, ⸚e	exit (*of actor*)
der Anschlag, ⸚e	notice, poster
der Auftritt, -e	scene (*as in* "Act I, scene 2")
der Ausgang, ⸚e	exit, way out
der Balkon*, -s *or* -e	(dress) circle
der Eingang, ⸚e	entrance, way in
der Eintritt, -e	entrance (*of actor onto stage*)
der Rang	circle (*in theatre*)
der erste Rang	dress circle
der zweite Rang	upper circle
der Schauspieler	actor
der (Sitz)platz, ⸚e	seat
der Star*, -s	star (*male or female*)
der Theaterzettel	programme (*leaflet*)
der Vorhang, ⸚e	curtain

* THEATER (f)

die Aufführung, -en	performance
die Bühne, -n	stage, platform
die Bühnendekoration	scenery
die Karte*, -n	ticket
die Komödie, -n	comedy
die Musik	music
die Pause*, -n	interval
die Person*, -en	character (*in play*)
die Rolle*, -n	role, part
die Schauspielerin	actress
die Show, -s	show
die Szene, -n	scene; stage
die (Theater)karte, -n	(theatre) ticket
die (Theater)kasse, -n	box office
die Tragödie, -n	tragedy
die Vorführung, -en	showing
die Vorstellung, -en	performance, show

* THEATER (*nt*)

das Auftreten	entrance (*of actor*); performance (*of actor*)
das Drama, Dramen	drama
das Foyer	foyer
das Haus, Häuser	house
das Kostüm, -e	costume
das Lustspiel, -e	comedy
das Orchester*	orchestra
das Parkett*, -e	stalls
das Stück*, -e	play
das Theater	theatre
das (Theater)stück, -e	play
das Trauerspiel, -e	tragedy

ein Stück geben to put on a play
eine Rolle spielen to play a part
die Hauptrolle spielen to play the lead
die Vorstellung ist ausverkauft we have a full house, we have sold out
Meine Damen und Herren Ladies and gentlemen
der Vorhang geht auf/fällt the curtain rises/falls
klatschen, Beifall geben to clap, applaud
sich verbeugen to bow, take a bow

** TrHEATER *(m)*

der Applaus,	
der Beifall	applause
der Dramatiker	dramatist, playwright
der Regisseur	producer
der Schwank, ⸚e	farce
der Text, -e	script
die Zuhörer *(pl)*	audience *(listeners)*
die Zuschauer* *(pl)*	audience *(viewers)*

** THEATER *(f)*

die Besetzung	cast; casting *(of role)*
die Garderobe*, -n	cloakroom; wardrobe
die Inszenierung	production *(show)*
die Loge, -n	box
die Oper, -n	opera; opera house
die Platzanweiserin	usherette, attendant
die Regie	production *(theatre)*; direction *(cinema)*
die Reservierung	booking
die Theatergruppe, -n	dramatic society
die Tribüne*, -n	platform
die Vorhalle, -n	foyer
die Zugabe, -n	encore

** THEATER *(nt)*

das Plakat*, ⸚e	poster, notice
das Spiel(en)*	acting

*** THEATER (m)

der Inspizient	stage manager
der Intendant, -e	stage manager
der Orchesterraum, (-räume)	orchestra pit
der Produzent*	(film) producer
der Souffleur	prompter
der Spielleiter	stage manager·

*** THEATER (f)

die Galerie	'the gods', gallery
die Generalprobe, -n	dress rehearsal
die Handlung, -en	plot
die Kapelle, -n	band (music)
die Kulissen (pl)	wings; scenery
die Posse, -n	farce
die Probe, -n	rehearsal
die Souffleuse	prompter
die Vorverkaufkasse, -n	booking office
die Vorverkaufstelle, -n	booking agency
die Zuhörerschaft	audience

*** THEATER (nt)

das Kriminalstück, -e	thriller
das Opernglas (sg)	(pair of) opera glasses
das Rampenlicht (sg)	footlights
das Scheinwerferlicht, -er	spotlight

an der Vorverkaufkasse at the booking office
bei or in der Vorverkaufstelle at the booking agency
theatralisch theatrical

---

* TIERE—EINIGE MERKMALE (*m*)

der Elefant, -en	elephant
der Hals, ¨e	neck; throat
der Hund, -e	dog
der Löwe, -n	lion
der Ochse, -n	ox
der Schwanz, ¨e	tail
der Tiergarten, ¨	zoo, zoological gardens
der Tiger	tiger
der Zoo, -s	zoo

* TIERE—EINIGE MERKMALE (*f*)

die Hündin	bitch, (she-)dog
die Katze, -n	cat
die Kuh, ¨e	cow
die Löwin	lioness
die Maus, Mäuse	mouse
die Pfote, -n	paw (*small*)
die Ratte, -n	rat
die Tigerin	tigress
die Ziege, -n	(nanny-)goat

* TIERE—EINIGE MERKMALE (*nt*)

das Bein, -e	leg
das Haustier, -e	pet
das Maul, Mäuler	mouth
das Ohr, -en	ear
das Pferd, -e	horse
das Schaf, -e	sheep
das Schwein, -e	pig
das Tier, -e	animal

zahm tame; **wild** wild; **gehorsam** obedient
laufen to run
hüpfen to hop; **hoppeln** to hop (about)
springen to jump
schleichen to slink
kriechen to slither, crawl
einen Satz machen to spring (*of tiger etc*)
hochspringen to jump up
trompeten to trumpet
fressen to eat
beißen to bite
jagen to hunt; to shoot
auf die Fuchsjagd gehen to go fox-hunting
eine Falle aufstellen to set a trap
in die Falle gehen to be caught in a trap, be trapped
einen Frosch im Hals haben to have a frog in one's throat
'Warnung vor dem Hunde' 'beware of the dog'
der Hund wedelt mit dem Schwanz the dog wags its tail
der Wachhund watchdog
Platz!, sitz! down!
leg dich! lie down!
Männchen machen to sit up and beg; **Pfötchen geben** to give a paw
der Löwe ist aus dem Zoo entlaufen the lion escaped from the zoo
ein Tier freilassen to set an animal free
die Katze streicheln to stroke the cat
die Pfote ausstrecken to stretch out (its) paw
das Vorderbein foreleg
das Hinterbein hind leg
die Ohren aufstellen to prick up (its) ears
zu Pferd on horseback
reiten gehen to go riding
das Pferd schlägt aus the horse kicks
einen Kater haben to have a hangover
der Stierkampf bullfight
die Krallen zeigen/einziehen to put out/draw in (its) claws

** TIERE—EINIGE MERKMALE (m)

der Affe, -n	monkey
der Bär, -en	bear
der Bock, ̈e	buck, ram
der Bulle, -n	bull
der Esel	donkey
der Frosch, ̈e	frog
der Fuchs, ̈e	fox
der Hamster	hamster
der Hase, -n	hare
der Kater	tomcat
der Stier, -e	bull
der Streifen	stripe (of zebra)
der Wolf, ̈e	wolf

** TIERE—EINIGE MERKMALE (f)

die Fledermaus, (-mäuse)	bat
die Giraffe, -n	giraffe
die Pranke, -n	paw (large)
die Schlange*, -n	snake
die Tatze, -n	paw (small)

** TIERE—EINIGE MERKMALE (nt)

das Eichhörnchen	squirrel
das Haar, -e	hair
das Kamel	camel
das Känguruh, -s	kangaroo
das Kaninchen	rabbit
das Merkmal, -e	characteristic
das Pony, -s	pony
das Zebra, -s	zebra

*** TIERE—EINIGE MERKMALE (m)

der **Beutel**	pouch (of *kangaroo*)
der **Eisbär**, -en	polar bear
der **Hirsch**, -e	deer; stag
der **Höcker**	hump (of *camel*)
der **Huf**, -e	hoof
der **Igel**	hedgehog
der **Maulwurf**, ¨e	mole
der **Pelz**, -e	coat, fur
der **Rückenschild**, -e	shell (of *tortoise*)
der **Rüssel**	snout (of *pig*); trunk (of *elephant*)
der **Seehund**, -e	seal
der **Stachel**	spine (of *hedgehog*)
der **Stoßzahn**, ¨e	tusk
der **Wal(fisch)**, -e	whale
der **Ziegenbock**, ¨e	(billy)goat, he-goat

*** TIERE—EINIGE MERKMALE (f)

die **Falle**, -n	trap
die **Kralle**, -n	claw
die **Kröte**, -n	toad
die **Mähne**, -n	mane
die **Natter**, -n	adder, viper
die **Robbe**, -n	seal
die **Schildkröte**, -n	tortoise
die **Schnauze**, -n	snout, muzzle

*** TIERE—EINIGE MERKMALE (nt)

das **Fell**, -e	coat, fur
das **Flußpferd**, -e	hippopotamus
das **Geweih** (sg)	antlers
das **Horn**, ¨er	horn
das **Hufeisen**	horse-shoe
das **Krokodil**, -e	crocodile
das **Maultier**, -e	mule
das **Meerschweinchen**	guinea pig
das **Nashorn**, ¨er	rhinoceros
das **Nilpferd**, -e	hippopotamus
das **Reh**, -e	roe deer
das **Rhinozeros**, -se	rhinoceros

TIERAUFENTHALTSORTE

	ANIMALS HOMES
der **Adler** (eagle)	der **Adlerhorst** (eyrie)
der **Bär** (bear)	die **Bärenhöhle** (den)
die **Biene** (bee)	der **Bienenstock** (beehive)
der **Dachs** (badger)	der **Dachsbau** (sett)
der **Goldfisch** (goldfish)	das **Aquarium** (goldfish bowl)
die **Henne** (hen)	der **Hühnerstall**, das **Hühnerhaus** (henhouse)
der **Hund** (dog)	die **Hundehütte** (kennel)
das **Kaninchen** (rabbit)	die **Kaninchenhöhle**, der **Kaninchenbau** (burrow)
	der **Hasenstall** (hutch)
die **Kuh** (cow)	der **Kuhstall** (cowshed, byre)
der **Löwe** (lion)	die **Löwenhöhle** (den, lair)
der **Wellensittich** (budgie)	der **Käfig** (cage)
das **Pferd** (horse)	der **Pferdestall** (stable)
das **Schaf** (sheep)	der **Pferch**, der **Schafstall** (sheep-pen, sheep-fold)
das **Schwein** (pig)	der **Schweinestall** (pig-sty)
der **Vogel** (bird)	das **Nest** (nest)

TIERJUNGE UND TIERLAUTE

die **Ente** (duck)	das **Entchen** (duckling)	**quaken** (to quack); quak! (quack!)
das **Esel** (donkey)	das **Eselchen**	**schreien** (to bray); 'i'ah! (hee-haw!)

TIERJUNGE UND TIERLAUTE *(Forts)*

der Fuchs (fox)	**das Füchschen** (fox cub)	bellen *(to bark)*; kläffen *(to yelp)*
die Gans (goose)	**das Gänschen** (gosling)	gackern, schnattern *(to cackle)*; zischen *(to hiss)*; schreien *(to honk)*
das Huhn (hen) **die Henne**	**das Küken** (chicken, chick)	krähen *(to crow)*; glucken, locken *(to cluck)*; piepsen *(to cheep)*; kikeri'ki! *(cock-a-doodle-doo!)*
der Hund (dog)	**der kleine Hund** (puppy)	bellen *(to bark)*; kläffen *(to yap, yelp)*; knurren *(to growl)*; wau'wau! *(bow-wow!)*
die Katze (cat)	**das Kätzchen** (kitten)	schnurren *(to purr)*; miauen *(to miaow)*; miau! *(miaow!)*
der Löwe (lion)	**der junge Löwe** (lion cub)	brüllen *(to roar)*
das Pferd (horse)	**das Fohlen** (foal)	wiehern *(to neigh)*
die Rinder *(pl)* (cow) **die Kuh**	**das Kalb** (calf)	brüllen *(to bellow)*; muhen *(to moo)*; muh! *(moo!)*
das Schaf (sheep)	**das Lamm** (lamb)	blöken *(to bleat)*; mäh! *(baa!)*
das Schwein (pig)	**das Ferkel** (piglet)	grunzen *(to grunt)*; quiek! *(oink, oink!)*
die Ziege (goat)	**das Kitz** (kid)	meckern *(to bleat)*; mäh! *(meee!)*

* VÖGEL (m)

der Hahn*, ⸚e	cock
der Spatz, -en,	
der Sperling, -e	sparrow
der Vogel, ⸚	bird

** VÖGEL (m)

der Adler	eagle
der Fink, -en	finch
der Flügel*	wing
der Kanarienvogel, ⸚	canary
der Kuckuck, -e	cuckoo
der Papagei, -en	parrot
der Schwan, ⸚e	swan
der Star*, -e	starling
der Wellensittich	budgie, budgerigar

*** VÖGEL (m)

der Eisvogel, ⸚	kingfisher
der Falke, -n	falcon
der Fasan, -e(n)	pheasant
der Flamingo	flamingo
der Geier	vulture
der Habicht. -e	hawk
der Hirtenstar, -s	mynah bird
der Pfau, -en	peacock
der Pinguin, -e	penguin
der Puter	turkey(-cock)
der Rabe, -n	raven
der Schnabel, ⸚	beak, bill
der Specht, -e	woodpecker
der Storch, ⸚e	stork
der Strauß*, Strauße	ostrich
der Truthahn, ⸚e	turkey

zwitschern to twitter; singen to sing
die Vögel schlagen mit den Flügeln birds flap
  their wings; fliegen to fly
sie bauen ein Nest they build a nest
Eier legen to lay (its) eggs

* VÖGEL (f)

die Amsel	blackbird
die Ente, -n	duck
die Gans, ⸚e	goose
die Henne, -n	hen
die Lerche, -n	lark
die Luft	air
die Taube, -n	dove, pigeon

** VÖGEL (f)

die Drossel, -n	thrush
die Eule, -n	owl
die Feder*, -n	feather
die Krähe, -n	crow
die Möwe, -n	(sea)gull
die Nachtigall, -en	nightingale
die Schwalbe, -n	swallow

*** VÖGEL (f)

die Blaumeise, -n	bluetit
die Dohle, -n	jackdaw
die Elster, -n	magpie
die Saatkrähe, -n	rook

*, **, *** VÖGEL (nt)

das Huhn, ⸚er	chicken, fowl
das Nest -er	nest
das Rotkehlchen	robin (redbreast)
das schottische Moorhuhn, -n ⸚er	grouse
das Vogelschutzgebiet, -e	bird sanctuary

Nester ausnehmen to go bird-nesting
in die Höhe fliegen to soar, fly upwards
federleicht as light as a feather
zwei Fliegen mit einer Klappe schlagen to kill two
  birds with one stone
in der Vogelfluglinie as the crow flies

* WELTALL (*m*)

der Ausländer	foreigner
der Berg*, -e	hill, mountain
der Fluß, ⸚sse	river
der Forst, -e	forest
der Hügel	hill
der Mond, -e	moon
der Planet, -en	planet
der See, -n	lake
der Stern, -e	star
der Strom, ⸚e	river
der Wald, ⸚er	forest, wood

nach Norden (*m*)	to the north
nach Süden (*m*)	to the south
nach Osten (*m*)	to the east
nach Westen (*m*)	to the west

* WELTALL (*f*)

die Ausländerin	foreigner
die Erde	the earth
die Gegend, -en	region, area
die Hauptstadt, ⸚e	capital (city); chief town, county town
die Karte*, -n	map
die Küste, -n	coast
die Landkarte, -n	map
die Nation, -en	nation
die Nationalität, -en	nationality
die See, -n	sea
die Welt, -en	world
die Weltkarte, -n	map of the world
die Wüste, -n	desert

* WELTALL (*nt*)

im/ins Ausland	abroad
das Land*, ⸚er	country
das Meer, -e	ocean; sea
das Volk, ⸚er	people, nation
das Weltall	universe

** WELTALL (m)

der (Berg)gipfel	mountain peak, mountain top
der Gebirgszug, ⁓e	mountain range or chain
der Horizont	horizon
der Kanal*, Kanäle	canal
der Kontinent, -e	continent
der Landsmann, (-leute)	compatriot, fellow countryman
der Nordpol	North Pole
der Ozean, -e	ocean
der Südpol	South Pole

** WELTALL (f)

die Antarktik	the Antarctic
die Arktik	the Arctic
die Bevölkerung	population
die Ebene, -n	plain
die Gebirgskette, -n	mountain range or chain
die Grenze, -n	border, frontier
die Insel	island
die Landsmännin, (-leute)	compatriot, fellow countrywoman
die (Mutter)sprache, -n	(native) language
eine Provinz	a province
die Provinz (pl)	the provinces

** WELTALL (nt)

das Plateau, -s	plateau
das Tal, ⁓er	valley

eine Weltreise machen to go round the world
das höchste/größte/schönste der Welt the highest/biggest/most beautiful in the world
die Welt ist klein! it's a small world!
ferne Länder far-off countries
aus welchem Land kommen Sie? what country do you come from?
die Dritte Welt the Third World
die Entwicklungsländer the developing countries

*** WELTALL *m*

der Äquator	equator
der Globus, Globen	
or -se	globe
der Vulkan, -e	volcano
der Wendekreis (des	
Krebses/des	
Steinbocks)	tropic (of Cancer/of
	Capricorn)

*** WELTALL (*f*)

die Erdkugel	globe, earth
die Halbinsel	peninsula
die Milchstraße	the galaxy, the Milky
	Way
die Mündung, -en	estuary, mouth (*of river*)
die Rasse, -n	race
die Schlucht, -en	gorge
die Tropen (*pl*)	the Tropics

*** WELTALL (*nt*)

das Erdbeben	earthquake
das Festland, ˝er	continent; mainland
das Heimatland, ˝er	native country
das Tafelland, ˝er	plateau, tableland

* WERKZEUGE *(m)*

der Draht, ⸚e	wire
der Faden, ⸚	thread
der Flaschenöffner	bottle opener
der Hammer	hammer
der Nagel, ⸚	nail
der Schlüssel	key

* WERKZEUGE *(f)*

die Leiter, -n	ladder
die Maschine, -n	machine
die Säge, -n	saw
die Schere, -n	(pair of) scissors
die Schnur*, ⸚e	string; wire, flex

* WERKZEUGE *(nt)*

das Gummi(band), -s and (⸚er)	rubber band, elastic band
das Kabel	wire; cable
das Schloß*, ⸚sser	lock

flicken to mend, repair
reparieren to repair (*machine*)
sägen to saw; **durchsägen** to saw through
hämmern to hammer
schrauben to screw; **aufschrauben, losschrauben** to unscrew
klopfen to tap, bang; **lösen** to loosen
schneiden to cut; **stopfen** to darn
brauchen to need
benutzen to use
ein Stück Holz entzweisägen to saw a piece of wood in two
einen Nagel in die Wand schlagen to hammer a nail into the wall
etwas in etwas einschrauben to screw something into something
auf eine Leiter steigen to climb a ladder
die Leiter gegen die Wand lehnen to lean the ladder against the wall

** WERKZEUGE (m)

der Baugrund, ⁇e	construction site, building site
der Kleb(e)streifen	adhesive tape
der Pinsel*	paintbrush
der Reißnagel, ⁇	drawing pin, thumbtack
der Spaten	spade
der Strang, ⁇e	
der Strick, -e	rope
der Tesafilm	sellotape, adhesive tape

** WERKZEUGE (f)

die Baustelle, -n	building site, construction site
die Fertigungshalle, -n	workshop
die Harke, -n	rake
die Heftzwecke, -n	drawing pin, thumbtack
die Nadel, -n	needle
die Planke, -n	plank
die Reißzwecke, -n	drawing pin, thumbtack
die Schraube, -n	screw
die Werkstatt, ⁇en	workshop

, * WERKZEUGE (nt)

das Bohrgerät, -e	drill
das Brett*, -er	plank, board
das Do-it-yourself	do-it-yourself, D.I.Y.
das Gerüst, -e	scaffolding
das Seil, -e,	
das Tau, -e	rope
das Vorhängeschloß, ⁇sser	
das Vorlegeschloß, ⁇sser	padlock
das Werkzeug, -e	tool

ein Zimmer tapezieren/streichen to paper/paint a
room
'frisch gestrichen' 'wet paint'
'Betreten der Baustelle verboten' 'building site:
keep out'
(gerne) basteln to be handy with one's hands

*** WERKZEUGE (m)

der Bastler	handyman
der Beitel	chisel
der Bohrer	drill
der Büchsenöffner,	
der Dosenöffner	tin opener
der Hobel	plane
der Hohlspatel	trowel (for gardening)
der Holzhammer	mallet
der Klebstoff, -e	glue
der Korkenzieher	corkscrew
der Nähkasten	needlework box
der Pflanzenheber	trowel (for gardening)
der Pickel	pick, pickaxe
der Preßluftbohrer	pneumatic drill
der Schraubenschlüssel	spanner
der Schraubenzieher	screwdriver
der Schraubstock, ⁈e	vice
der Stacheldraht	barbed wire
der Werkzeugkasten	tool chest, tool box

*** WERKZEUGE (f)

die Drahtzange, -n	pliers
die Feder*, -n	spring, coil
die Feile, -n	file
die Gabel, -n	fork
die Hacke*, -n	pickaxe; hoe
die Kelle, -n	trowel (for building)
die Kneifzange, -n	pliers, tongs
die Kreuzhacke, -n	pick
die Libelle*, -n	spirit level
die Maurerkelle, -n	trowel (for building)
die Nivellierwaage, -n	spirit level
die Picke, -n	pick, pickaxe
die Schaufel, -n	shovel
die Sense, -n	scythe
die Trittleiter, -n	stepladder
die Wasserwaage, -n	spirit level
die Zange, -n	pliers; tongs

* WETTER (*m*)

der Blitz, -e	lightning, flash of lightning
der (dicke) Nebel	fog
der Donner	thunder
der Donnerschlag, ⁓e	thunderclap
der Himmel	sky; heaven
der Mond	moon
der Nebel	mist; fog
der Rauch	smoke
der Regen	rain
der (Regen)schirm, -e	umbrella
der Schatten	shadow; shade
der Schnee	snow
der Schneeball, ⁓e	snowball
der Schneemann, -männer	snowman
der Sonnenschein	sunshine
der Stern, -e	star
der Wetterbericht	weather report
der Wind, -e	wind
der Windstoß, ⁓e	gust of wind

* WETTER (*f*)

die Finsternis	darkness
die Flut, -en	flood
die Hitze	heat
die Jahreszeit, -en	season
die Kälte	cold
die Luft	air
die Natur	Nature
die Sonne	sun
die Welt	world
die Wolke, -n	cloud

* WETTER (*nt*)

das Eis*	ice
das Gewitter	storm, thunderstorm
das Licht, -er	light
das Unwetter	storm, tempest
das Wetter	weather

** WETTER (m)

der **Frost**, ⸚e	frost
der **Hagel**	hail
der **Mondschein**	moonlight
der **Regenbogen**	rainbow
der **Schneefall**, ⸚e	snowfall
der **Smog**	smog
der **Sonnenschirm**, -e	parasol
der **Sonnenstrahl**, -en	ray of sunshine
der **Staub**	dust
der **Sturm**, ⸚e	storm, tempest, gale

** WETTER (f)

die **Atmosphäre**	atmosphere
die **Dämmerung**	twilight, dusk; dawn
die **(Morgen)dämmerung**	dawn
die **Wettervorhersage**, -n	weather forecast

** WETTER (nt)

das **Halbdunkel**	twilight, dusk; semi-darkness
das **Klima**, -s	climate
das **Mondlicht**	moonlight
das **Zwielicht**	twilight, dusk; semi-darkness

blitzen to flash (*lightning*) (es blitzt)
donnern to thunder (es donnert)
scheinen to shine (die Sonne/der Mond scheint)
(stark) regnen to rain (hard) (es regnet)
gießen to pour (es gießt)
schneien to snow (es schneit)
blasen, wehen to blow (der Wind bläst/weht)
tauen to thaw (es tauet)
schmelzen to melt (der Schnee schmilzt)
frieren to freeze (es friert)
stürmen to be stormy (es stürmt)
wie ist das Wetter heute? what's the weather like today?
wie ist das Wetter bei euch? what's the weather like with you?

*** WETTER (m)

der **Blitzableiter**	lightning conductor
der **Dunst**	haze
der **Eiszapfen**	icicle
der **Gefrierpunkt**	freezing point
der **Luftzug, ¨e**	draught
der **Orkan, -e**	hurricane
der **Planet, -en**	planet
der **Platzregen**	shower, downpour
der **Regenguß, (-güsse)**	downpour
der **Regentropfen**	raindrop
der **Schaden, ¨**	damage
der **Schauer**	shower
der **Schneepflug, ¨e**	snowplough
der **Schneeregen**	sleet
der **Sonnenaufgang, ¨e**	sunrise
der **Sonnenuntergang, ¨e**	sunset
der **Tagesanbruch**	dawn, break of day
der **Tau**	dew
der **Weltraum**	space
der **Zug*, ¨e**	draught

warm warm; **kühl** cool
heiß hot; **kalt** cold
schön lovely; **schrecklich** terrible
mild mild; **rauh** harsh
sonnig sunny; **windig** windy
stürmisch stormy; **neb(e)lig** misty, foggy
schwül close, thundery; **feucht** damp
der **Himmel ist bedeckt/bewölkt** the sky is over-
cast/cloudy
im Schatten in the shade, in the shadows
im Freien in the open air
der **Blitz schlägt (in das Haus/in den Baum) ein**
lightning strikes (the house/the tree)
vom Blitz getroffen struck by lightning

*** WETTER (f)

die **Aufheiterungen** (pl)	bright periods
die **Bö**, -en	squall, gust of wind
die **Brise**, -n	breeze
die **Dürre**, -n	drought
die **Hitzewelle**, -n	heatwave
die **Lache**, -n	puddle, pool
die **Pfütze**, -n	puddle
die **Schneeflocke**, -n	snowflake
die **Schneewehe**, -n	snowdrift
die **Trockenheit**	drought
die **Über-** schwemmung, -en	flood, deluge

*** WETTER (nt)

das **Barometer**	barometer
das **Erdbeben**	earthquake
das **Glatteis**	black ice
das **Morgengrauen**	dawn
das **Schneegestöber**	flurry of snow
das **Tauwetter**	thaw

beim **Sonnenaufgang/Sonnenuntergang** at sunrise/ sunset
die **Sonne geht auf/geht unter** the sun rises/sets
die **Sonne strahlt** the sun is beaming
es **dunkelt, es wird dunkel** it is growing dark
es **fängt an zu schneien** it is beginning to snow
naß werden to get wet
eine **vereiste Stelle** a patch of black ice
so ein **Hundewetter!** what awful weather!

ZAHLEN UND MENGEN

der Becher (Joghurt)	pot (of yogurt)
ein bißchen	a little (bit of)
die Büchse*	tin, can
der or das Deziliter	decilitre
das Dutzend	dozen
Dutzende von	dozens of
etwas	a little (bit of)
das Faß	barrel
die Flasche (Wein)	bottle (of wine)
das Glas* (Milch)	glass (of milk)
das Glas* Marmelade	jar or pot of jam
eine Halbe	a half (litre of beer *etc*)
ein halbes Dutzend/ Pfund	half-a-dozen/-pound, a half dozen/pound
ein halbes Kilo/Liter	half a kilo/litre
die Handvoll (Münzen)	handful (of coins)
der Haufen	heap, pile
ein Haufen	heaps of
Hunderte von	hundreds of
hundert Gramm Käse	a hundred grammes of cheese
die Kanne (Kaffee)	pot (of coffee)
das Kilo(gramm)	kilo(gramme)
ein Kleines	a half pint (*of beer etc*)
das Knäuel Wolle, das Wollknäuel	ball of wool
das Liter	litre
die Menge	crowd; heaps of
das Meter (Stoff)	metre (of cloth)
das Paar* (Schuhe)	pair (of shoes)
das Päckchen	packet
die Packung Keks/ Zigaretten	packet of biscuits/ cigarettes
das Pfund (Kartoffeln)	pound (of potatoes)
die Portion (Eis)	portion or helping (of ice cream)
der Riegel Seife/ Schokolade	cake or bar of soap/ chocolate

ZAHLEN UND MENGEN (Forts)

die Schachtel	box; packet (of cigarettes)
die Schar	group, band
die Scheibe (Brot)	slice (of bread)
die Schüssel	bowl, dish
der Stapel	pile
das Stück* Zucker	lump of sugar
das Stück* Kuchen	piece or slice of cake
das Stück* Papier	bit or piece of paper
die Tafel* Schokolade	bar of chocolate
die Tasse(voll)	cup(ful)
Tausende von	thousands of
der Teller	plate
das Viertel(pfund)	quarter(-pound)
ein wenig	a little (bit) of
der Würfel Zucker	lump of sugar
der Würfel Margarine	half a pound of margarine (in cube shape)

dem Dutzend/dem Hundert/dem Tausend nach by the dozen/the hundred/the thousand

für das Dutzend/das Hundert/das Tausend per dozen/hundred/thousand, (for) a dozen/a hundred/a thousand

1 KARDINALZAHLEN   CARDINAL NUMBERS

nought	0	null
one	1	eins
two	2	zwei
three	3	drei
four	4	vier
five	5	fünf
six	6	sechs
seven	7	sieben
eight	8	acht
nine	9	neun
ten	10	zehn
eleven	11	elf
twelve	12	zwölf
thirteen	13	dreizehn
fourteen	14	vierzehn
fifteen	15	fünfzehn
sixteen	16	sechzehn
seventeen	17	siebzehn
eighteen	18	achtzehn
nineteen	19	neunzehn
twenty	20	zwanzig
twenty-one	21	einundzwanzig
twenty-two	22	zweiundzwanzig
twenty-three	23	dreiundzwanzig
thirty	30	dreißig
thirty-one	31	einunddreißig
thirty-two	32	zweiunddreißig
forty	40	vierzig
fifty	50	fünfzig
sixty	60	sechzig
seventy	70	siebzig
eighty	80	achtzig
ninety	90	neunzig
ninety-nine	99	neunundneunzig
a (or one) hundred	100	hundert

KARDINALZAHLEN *(Forts)*

a hundred and one	101	hunderteins
a hundred and two	102	hundertzwei
a hundred and ten	110	hundertzehn
a hundred and eighty-two	182	hundertzweiundachtzig
two hundred	200	zweihundert
two hundred and one	201	zweihunderteins
two hundred and two	202	zweihundertzwei
three hundred	300	dreihundert
four hundred	400	vierhundert
five hundred	500	fünfhundert
six hundred	600	sechshundert
seven hundred	700	siebenhundert
eight hundred	800	achthundert
nine hundred	900	neunhundert
a *(or* one) thousand	1000	(ein)tausend
a thousand and one	1001	tausendeins
a thousand and two	1002	tausendzwei
two thousand	2000	zweitausend
ten thousand	10 000	zehntausend
a *(or* one) hundred thousand	100 000	hunderttausend
a *(or* one) million	1 000 000	eine Million
two million	2 000 000	zwei Millionen

1979 neunzehnhundertneunundsiebzig *or*
tausendneunhundertneunundsiebzig

gerade/ungerade Zahlen even/odd numbers
50 Prozent 50 per cent

2 ORDINALZAHLEN   ORDINAL NUMBERS

These can be masculine, feminine or neuter, and take the appropriate endings.

first	der Erste
second	der Zweite
third	der Dritte
fourth	der Vierte
fifth	der Fünfte
sixth	der Sechste
seventh	der Siebente
eighth	der Achte
ninth	der Neunte
tenth	der Zehnte
eleventh	der Elfte
twelfth	der Zwölfte
thirteenth	der Dreizehnte
fourteenth	der Vierzehnte
fifteenth	der Fünfzehnte
sixteenth	der Sechzehnte
seventeenth	der Siebzehnte
eighteenth	der Achtzehnte
nineteenth	der Neunzehnte
twentieth	der Zwanzigste
twenty-first	der Einundzwanzigste
twenty-second	der Zweiundzwanzigste
thirtieth	der Dreißigste
thirty-first	der Einunddreißigste
fortieth	der Vierzigste
fiftieth	der Fünfzigste
sixtieth	der Sechzigste
seventieth	der Siebzigste
eightieth	der Achtzigste
ninetieth	der Neunzigste
hundredth	der Hundertste

ORDINALZAHLEN *(Forts)*

hundred and first	der Hunderterste
hundred and tenth	der Hundertzehnte
two hundredth	der Zweihundertste
three hundredth	der Dreihundertste
four hundredth	der Vierhundertste
five hundredth	der Fünfhundertste
six hundredth	der Sechshundertste
seven hundredth	der Siebenhundertste
eight hundredth	der Achthundertste
nine hundredth	der Neunhundertste
thousandth	der Tausendste
two thousandth	der Zweitausendste
millionth	der Million(s)te
two millionth	der Zweimillion(s)te

zum zigsten Male for the umpteenth time
ein Millionär a millionaire

3 BRÜCHE / FRACTIONS

a half	halb, die Hälfte
one and a half kilos	eineinhalb Kilos, anderthalb Kilos
two and a half kilos	zweieinhalb Kilos
a third	ein Drittel *(nt)*
two thirds	zwei Drittel
a quarter	ein Viertel *(nt)*
three quarters	drei Viertel
a sixth	ein Sechstel *(nt)*
five and five sixths	fünf und fünfsechstel
an eighth	ein Achtel *(nt)*
a twelfth	ein Zwölftel *(nt)*
a twentieth	ein Zwanzigstel *(nt)*
a hundredth	ein Hundertstel *(nt)*
a thousandth	ein Tausendstel *(nt)*
a millionth	ein Millionstel *(nt)*

(0, 4) Null Komma vier (0.4) nought point four
die Flasche war dreiviertel leer the bottle was three-quarters empty

* ZEIT (m)	
der Abend, -e	evening
der Augenblick, -e	moment, instant
um Mittag	at mid-day, at noon
der Moment, -e	moment
der Monat, -e	month
der Morgen	morning
der Nachmittag	afternoon
der Tag, -e	day
der Vormittag	morning

* ZEIT (adv)	
vorgestern	the day before yesterday
gestern	yesterday
am vorigen or	the day before, the
vorgehenden Tag	previous day
heute	today
heute abend	tonight
morgen	tomorrow
am nächsten or	
folgenden Tag	the next or following day
übermorgen	the day after tomorrow
am übernächsten Tag	two days later

morgens	in the morning
nachmittags	in the afternoon
abends	in the evening
nachts	at night, by night
tagsüber, am Tage	during the day
stündlich	hourly
täglich	daily
wöchentlich	weekly
monatlich	monthly
jährlich	annually

wieviel Uhr ist es?, wie spät ist es? what time is it?
der wievielte ist heute?, den wievielten haben wir heute? what date is it today?
heutzutage nowadays

* ZEIT *(f)*

die Armbanduhr, -en	(wrist) watch
die Epoche, -n	epoch, period
eine halbe Stunde	a half-hour, half-an-hour
die Minute, -n	minute
um Mitternacht	at midnight
die Nacht, ¨e	night; night-time
die Sekunde, -n	second
die Stunde*, -n	hour
die Tageszeit	daytime
die Uhr*, -en	clock; time
die Viertelstunde	quarter of an hour
die Woche, -n	week
die Zeit, -en	time

* ZEIT *(nt)*

das Datum, Daten	date
das Jahr, -e	year
das Jahrhundert, -e	century
das Mal, -e	time, occasion
das Wochenende, -n	weekend

die Uhr aufziehen to wind up the clock
die Uhr geht nach/vor/richtig the clock is slow/fast/right
früh early; **spät** late; **bald** soon; **später** later; **fast** almost, nearly
um 8 Uhr aufstehen to get up at 8 o'clock
es ist gerade *or* **punkt 2 Uhr** it is exactly 2 o'clock
halb 3 half past 2; **halb 9** half past 8
gegen 8 Uhr round about 8 o'clock
es ist Viertel nach 5/Viertel vor 5 it is a quarter past 5/a quarter to 5
pünktlich punctually
der Zug hat 20 Minuten Verspätung the train is 20 minutes late
warum kommst du so spät? why are you so late?
wir werden zu spät kommen we're going to be (too) late

** ZEIT (m)
der Kalender	calendar
der Zeitabschnitt, -e	time, period

** ZEIT (f)
die Essenszeit, -en	mealtime
die Gegenwart*	present (time); present (tense)
die Mittagspause	lunch break
die Vergangenheit	past (time); past (tense)
die Verspätung	lateness, delay (of vehicle)
die Zukunft	future (time); future (tense)

** ZEIT (nt)
das Futur(um)	future tense
das Mittelalter	the Middle Ages
das Präsens	present tense
das Zuspätkommen	lateness, late arrival (of person)

einen Augenblick! just a minute!
in diesem/dem Augenblick at this/that moment
im selben Augenblick at that very moment
ich habe keine Zeit (dazu) I have no time (for it)
(sich) die Zeit vertreiben to pass the time
es ist Zeit zum Essen it is time for lunch (dinner etc)
eine Zeitlang bleiben to stay for a while
anderthalb Stunden warten to wait an hour and a half
damals at that time
nie, niemals never; jemals ever
diesmal this time; **ein anderes Mal** another time
nächstes Mal next time
das erste/letzte Mal the first/last time
zum ersten/letzten Mal for the first/last time
am Wochenende at the weekend
über das Wochenende for the weekend
ich habe es eilig I'm in a hurry
ich habe keine Eile I'm in no hurry; **es ist nicht eilig, es hat keine Eile** there's no hurry

*** ZEIT *(m)*

der Einbruch der Nacht	nightfall
der Tagesanbruch	daybreak
der Uhrzeiger	hand *(of clock etc)*
vierzehn Tage	a fortnight
der Wecker	alarm clock
der Zeiger	hand *(of clock etc)*

*** ZEIT *(f)*

die Kuckucksuhr, -en	cuckoo clock
die Mittagszeit, -en	lunch time
die Pause*, -n	interval; pause; break
die Standuhr, -en	grandfather clock
die Stoppuhr, -en	stopwatch
zwei Wochen	a fortnight

*** ZEIT *(nt)*

das Jahrzehnt, -e	decade
das Schaltjahr, -e	leap year
das Zeitalter	age
das Zifferblatt, ¨er	face, dial *(of clock etc)*

vor einer Woche/einem Monat/2 Jahren a week/a month/2 years ago

gestern/heute vor einer Woche a week ago yesterday/today

gestern/heute vor 2 Jahren 2 years ago yesterday/today

letzten Donnerstag vor einem Monat a month last Thursday

in einer Woche/einem Monat/2 Jahren in a week('s time)/a month('s time)/2 years(' time)

morgen/heute in einer Woche a week tomorrow/today

morgen/heute in 2 Jahren 2 years tomorrow/today

am Donnerstag in einem Monat a month next Thursday, a month on Thursday

The vocabulary items on pages 208 to 234 have been grouped under parts of speech rather than themes because they can apply in a wide range of circumstances. Please use them just as freely as the nouns already given.

abgenutzt worn out (*object*)
abscheulich hideous
ähnlich (+ *dat*) similar (to), like
albern silly, foolish
allein alone
allerlei all kinds of
allgemein popular
alltäglich ordinary
alt old
amüsant amusing
andere(r, s) other
anders different
Anfangs- elementary
angenehm pleasant
angrenzend neighbouring
arm poor
artig well-behaved, good
aufgeregt excited
aufgeweckt alive, lively
aufrichtig sincere
augenscheinlich evident
ausführlich detailed, elaborate
ausgeschmückt (mit) decorated (with)
ausgestreckt stretched (out)
ausgezeichnet excellent
ausschließlich sole, exclusive
außerordentlich extra-

ordinary
bedauernswert pathetic, pitiful
befriedigt (von) satisfied (with), pleased (at)
begeistert keen, enthusiastic (about)
belebt busy (*street*)
belegt reserved (*seat*)
beleuchtet illuminated, flood-lit
beliebt popular
bemerkenswert striking
benachbart neighbouring
bereit ready
berühmt famous
beschäftigt (mit) busy (with) (*of person*)
besetzt engaged, taken
besondere(r, s) special
besorgt worried, anxious, troubled
beteiligt (an + *dat*) involved (in)
beunruhigt worried, disturbed
bevorzugt privileged
bewegt moved, touched
breit wide, broad
bunt colourful, gay
dankbar grateful
dauernd perpetual

delikat delicate; delicious
deutlich clear, sharp
dicht thick (*forest*)
dick thick
dickflüssig thick (*liquid*)
dringend urgent
dumm silly, stupid
dunkel dark
dünn thin
dynamisch dynamic
echt real, genuine
ehemalig old, former
ehrlich sincere, honest
eifrig keen, enthusiastic
eigen own
einfach simple, plain, easy; elementary
einheimisch native
einzeln single, individual
einzig alone, single; only (*child*)
elegant elegant, smart
elektrisch, Elektro- electric
elend poor, wretched
End- final
endgültig final, definite
endlos endless
eng narrow; tight (*clothes*)
entmutigt discouraged
entschlossen firm, determined
entsetzlich terrible
entzückend delightful
erfahren experienced
erfreulich enjoyable
erfreut delighted
ernst serious, solemn

ernsthaft serious, earnest
erreichbar reachable, within reach
erschaffen created, established
erschöpft exhausted; worn out
erstaunlich amazing, extraordinary
erstaunt astonished
Fach- technical
fähig capable
falsch false; wrong
faul lazy; rotten
feierlich solemn
fein fine
fern far, far-off
fertig prepared, ready
fest firm, hard
fett fat
finster dark
flach flat
fortgeschritten advanced
fortwährend continual, endless
frech cheeky
frei free, vacant; free (of charge)
frisch fresh; cool
furchtbar frightful
fürchterlich terrible
ganz whole, complete
geboren born
geduldig patient
geeignet suitable
gefährlich dangerous
gefroren frozen
geheim secret
geheimnisvoll mysterious

gemischt mixed, assorted
gemütlich comfortable
genau clear, exact; precise, strict
gerade straight
geringste(r, s) slightest, least
gesamt whole, entire, complete
geschichtlich historical
geteilt divided
gewaltig powerful, huge
gewalttätig violent
gewiß sure, certain
gewöhnlich usual, ordinary; common
gewöhnt (an + acc) accustomed (to)
glatt smooth
gleich same
glücklich happy, fortunate
gnädig worthy
gnädige Frau Madam
graziös graceful
grob coarse, rude
groß big, great, large; tall
großartig magnificent
Grund- primary
günstig suitable, convenient
gut good
gütig kind, nice
hart hard
häßlich ugly
Haupt- main
heftig strong, violent; furious

heimatlich native
heiß hot
hell pale; bright, light
herrlich delightful, marvellous
hervorragend magnificent
historisch historical
hoch high
höflich polite, civil
hübsch pretty
humorvoll humorous
illustriert illustrated
intelligent intelligent
interessant interesting
isoliert isolated
jede(r, s) each, every
jung young
kalt cold
kein no, not any
kindisch infantile, childish
kindlich childlike
klar clear, sharp
klatschnaß wet through, soaking wet
klein small, little
klug wise, clever
komisch funny, humorous
kompliziert complicated
körperlich physical
kostbar expensive; precious
kostenlos free
köstlich delicious
kräftig strong
kühl cool
kurz brief, short
lächelnd smiling

lächerlich ridiculous
lahm feeble (*excuse*)
Landes- national
lang long
langsam slow
langweilig boring
lärmend noisy
lästig annoying (*person*)
laut loud, noisy
lauter (*with pl*) nothing but, only
lebendig alive
lebhaft lively
lecker delicious
leer empty
leicht easy; light (*weight*)
leidenschaftlich passionate
leise quiet, soft, low
letzt last, latest; final
liebe(r, s) dear
Lieblings- favourite
linke(r, s) left
lustig gay
sich lustig machen über (+ *acc*) to make fun of
luxuriös luxurious
Luxus- luxury, luxurious
mächtig powerful, mighty
mager thin
mehrere several
merkwürdig strange, odd, remarkable
Militär-, militärisch military
mindeste least
mißtrauisch suspicious
mitleidig sympathetic, pitiful

modern modern
möglich possible
müde tired
munter gay
mutig courageous
mysteriös mysterious
nächste(r, s) next
nah near, close
natürlich natural; native
nett nice, charming
neu new
neuerlich recent
neu(e)st latest
neugierig curious
niedrig low
nötig necessary
notwendig necessary
nützlich useful
nutzlos useless, unnecessary
obligatorisch compulsory, obligatory
offen open; frank, sincere
offenbar, offensichtlich obvious
öffentlich public
offiziell official
ordentlich (neat and) tidy
Orts- local
pädagogisch educational
passend suitable
persönlich personal
populär popular
prächtig magnificent
praktisch practical
privat private; personal
privilegiert privileged
Quadrat-, quadratisch square

rauh rough; harsh
recht right
rege active, lively
reich rich
reif ripe
rein clean
reizend charming
religiös religious
reserviert reserved
richtig right, correct
riesig huge, gigantic
romantisch romantic
ruhig quiet, peaceful
rund round
sanft gentle, soft
satt full (*person*)
ich habe es satt I'm fed
up (with it)
sauber clean
scharf sharp; keen
schattig shady, dim
scheu shy
schick smart
schläfrig sleepy
schlank slender, slim
schlau cunning, sly
schlecht bad
schlimm bad
schmal narrow; slender
schmutzig dirty
schnell fast, quick, rapid
schockierend shocking
schockiert outraged
schön beautiful
schrecklich terrible;
frightful
schroff steep; jagged;
brusque
schüchtern shy
schweigsam silent

schwer heavy; serious
schwierig difficult
seltsam strange, odd,
curious
sicher sure; safe (and
sound)
sichtbar visible
solche such
Sonder- special
sonderbar strange, odd
sorgenfrei carefree
sorgfältig careful
spannend exciting
staatsbürgerlich civil
Stadt-, städtisch munici-
pal; urban
ständig perpetual
stark strong, hard
steif stiff
steil steep
still quiet, peaceful
stolz (auf + *acc*) proud
(of)
strahlend shining (*light*)
streng severe, harsh,
strict
süß sweet
sympathisch likeable
tapfer brave
technisch technical
tief deep
toll mad
tot dead
tragbar portable
traurig sad
treu true (*friend etc*)
trocken dry
typisch (für) typical (of)
übel wicked
überfüllt crowded

übrig left-over
unartig naughty, wicked
unbekannt unknown
uneben uneven
unerhört shocking
unerkannt unrecognized
unerträglich horrid,
unbearable
ungeheuer huge
ungezogen naughty
unglaublich unbelievable
unglücklich unhappy,
unfortunate
unheimlich weird,
sinister
unmöglich impossible
unterhaltend amusing,
entertaining
ursprünglich original
verantwortlich (für)
responsible (for)
verärgert annoyed
verboten prohibited,
forbidden
verehrt high,
distinguished
verlegen embarrassed,
awkward
verletzt injured
vernünftig sensible,
reasonable
verpflichtet obliged
verrückt mad
verschieden various,
different
verschiedene several
versehen (mit) provided
(with)
verständlich under-
standable

verwickelt complicated
in etwas verwickelt sein
to be involved in some-
thing
verwundert astonished,
amazed
viereckig square
volkstümlich popular (of
the people)
voll (+ gen) full (of)
vollkommen perfect,
complete
vollständig complete
vorderst front (row etc)
wach awake
wahr true
warm warm
weich soft
weise wise
weit far
welche? what?, which?
wert (+ gen) worthy (of)
wichtig important
wild fierce
wohlerzogen good, well-
behaved
wohlhabend well-off
wunderbar marvellous
würdig (+ gen) worthy
(of)
zähe tough
zahlreich numerous
zart gentle, tender
zeitgenössisch con-
temporary
zerstört destroyed
zig umpteen
zivil civil (not military)
zusätzlich extra

ADVERBIEN

Many other adverbs have the same form as the adjective

absichtlich deliberately, on purpose

allerdings certainly; of course, to be sure

anders otherwise; differently

außerdem besides

äußerst extremely

bald soon; almost

besser better

am besten best, best of all

bloß only

da there; here; then

daher from there; from that place

dahin (to) there; then

danach after that; afterwards

dann then

darin in it, in there

deshalb therefore, for that reason

dort there

dorthin (to) there, to that place

draußen out of doors; outside

drinnen inside; indoors

durchaus thoroughly, absolutely

eben exactly; just; precisely

eher sooner

am ehesten soonest

eigentlich really, actually, as a matter of fact

einmal once; one day; some day

auf einmal all at once; at the same time

endlich at last, finally

erst first; at first; only (time)

erstens first(ly), in the first place; to begin with

fast almost, nearly

freilich certainly, to be sure

früh early

ganz quite; completely, entirely

gegenwärtig at present, at the moment

genau exactly; just

genug enough

(nicht) gerade (not) just, (not) exactly

geradeaus straight ahead

gern(e) willingly; gladly

gewöhnlich usually, generally

glücklicherweise fortunately

gut well

häufig frequently

heutzutage nowadays, (in) these days

hier here

hierher this way, (to) here, to this place

hinten at the back, behind

höchst highly, extremely
hoffentlich I hope, hopefully
immer always
inzwischen meanwhile, in the meantime
irgendwo(hin) (to) somewhere (or other)
je ever
jedenfalls in any case
jedesmal each time, every time
jedesmal wenn whenever
je . . . desto: je mehr desto besser the more the better
jemals ever; at any time
jetzt now
kaum hardly, scarcely
keineswegs in no way; by no means
komischerweise funnily (enough), in a funny way
künftig in future
langsam slowly
leider unfortunately
lieber rather, preferably
am liebsten most (of all), best (of all)
links left, on or to the left
manchmal sometimes
mehr more
meinetwegen for my sake; on my behalf
am meisten most
meistens mostly, for the most part
merkwürdigerweise strange to say

mitten (in) in the middle or midst (of)
möglichst as possible
nachher after that, afterwards
neu newly; afresh, anew
neu füllen etc to refill etc
nichtsdestoweniger nevertheless
nie, niemals never
noch still; yet
noch einma. (once) again
normalerweise normally, in the normal course of events
nun now
nur only
oben above; upstairs
oft often
plötzlich suddenly
rechts right, on or to the right
regelmäßig regularly
richtig correctly; downright
rundherum round about, all (a)round, round and round
schlecht badly
schnell quickly
schrecklich terribly, awfully
sehr very, a lot, very much
selbst even
selten seldom, rarely
so so, thus, like this
sofort at once, immediately

sogar even
sogleich at once, immediately
sonst otherwise; or else
überall(hin) everywhere, in all directions
übrigens for the rest, otherwise; by the way
umher about, around
ungefähr about, approximately
unten below; downstairs; at the bottom
unterwegs on the way; under way
viel much, a lot of
vielleicht perhaps, maybe
völlig fully, thoroughly, perfectly *etc*
vorallem above all
vorbei along, by, past
vorher before, previously, beforehand

vorläufig temporarily; for the time being
wahrscheinlich probably
wann(?) when(?)
warum(?) why(?)
wie(?), wie! how(?), how!
wieder again
wo/woher/wohin/ wovon(?) where/from where/(to) where/from where(?)
z.B. (zum Beispiel) for example
ziemlich fairly, rather
zu too
zuerst first; first of all; at first
zufällig accidentally, by chance; as it happened
zurück back (to come back *etc*)
zweitens second(ly), in the second place

HAUPTWÖRTER

das Abenteuer adventure
die Abgabe, -n tax
der Abhang, ¨e slope
die Abkürzung, -en short-cut; abbreviation
der Abschnitt, -e section; paragraph
die Absicht, -en intention
die Abteilung, -en section, department
das Andenken memory; souvenir
der Anfang, ¨e beginning
der Angehörige, -n, die Angehörige, -n member
der Angst, ¨e fear
ich habe Angst (vor + dat) I am afraid or frightened (of)
die Anmeldung, -en notice
die Ansicht, -en view (towards)
die Anstalten preparations
die Antwort, -en reply
die Anweisungen instructions
die Anwesenheit, -en presence
das Anzeichen sign
die Anzeige, -n notice
der Apparat, -e machine
das Ärgernis, -se annoyance; boredom
die Art, -en way, method; kind, sort
der Aufenthalt, -e stay

die Aufmerksamkeit, -en attention
das Aufsehen stir
die Aufsicht, -en supervision
der Ausdruck, ¨e term, expression
die Auseinandersetzung, -en argument, dispute
der Ausgangspunkt, -e starting point
die Ausnahme, -n exception
die Äußerung, -en remark; expression
die Ausstellung, -en exhibition
die Auswahl, -en selection
der Bau, -e or **-ten** construction
die Beaufsichtigung, -en supervision
die Bedeutung, -en importance
die Bedingung, -en condition, stipulation
das Bedürfnis, -se need
der Befehl, -e order
die Begabung, -en talent
der Begriff: im Begriff sein, etwas zu tun to be busy doing something
das Beispiel, -e example
die Bemerkung, -en remark
die Bemühung, -en attempt, effort
die Berechnung, -en calculation

der Bescheid, -e message, information

sein Bestes tun to do one's best

der Betrag, "e sum

der Betrieb, -e works; bustle

das Bildnis, -se portrait

die Blödheit, -en stupidity

die Botschaft, -en message

das Botschaftsgebäude embassy

die Breite, -n width

der Bundestag West German Parliament

der Bursche, -n fellow

die Chance*, -n chance, opportunity

der Dank (sg) thanks

die Darstellung, -en version; representation

das Denken thought

das Diagramm, -e diagram

die Dicke, -n thickness; depth

der Dienst, -e service

die Dimension, -en dimension

das Ding, -e thing

die Disziplin, -en discipline

der Duft, "e smell, fragrance

die Dummheit, -en stupidity

der Dummkopf, "e idiot

der Dunst, "e fumes

das Eck, -e angle

die Ecke, -n corner

die Ehre, -n honour

die Einbildung, -en imagination

der Eindruck, "e impression

der Einfall, "e thought, idea

der Einspruch, "e claim

die Einwendung, -en objection

die Einzelheit, -en detail

die Eleganz elegance

der Empfang, "e reception

die Empfindung, -en feeling, emotion

das Ende, -n end

zu Ende gehen to end

die Entschlossenheit resolution

das Ereignis, -se event

die Erfahrung, -en experience

der Erfolg, -e result; success

das Ergebnis, -se result

die Erinnerung, -en memory; remembrance

die Erklärung, -en explanation

die Erkundigungen (fpl) information

die Erlaubnis, -se permission

die Erläuterung, -en explanation

das Erlebnis, -se experience

der **Ernst** earnestness, seriousness
das **Erstaunen** astonishment
die **Erwiderung, -en** retort
das **Exil, -e** exile (state)
die **Fassung, -en** version
der **Feind, -e** enemy
der **Feldherr, -en** general
das **Flüstern** whispering
die **Folge, -n** order; series; result
die **Form, -en** form, shape
die **Frage, -n** question
Fremde(r), -n, die Fremde, -n stranger; foreigner
die **Freude, -n** joy, pleasure
die **Freundlichkeit, -en** kindness
der **Frieden** peace
die **Frische** freshness; cool(ness)
der **Führer** guide, leader
die **Gebühr, -en** fees; tax
das **Gedächtnis, -se** memory
der **Gedanke, -n** thought, idea
das **Gedeihen** prosperity
die **Geduld** patience
die **Gefahr, -en** danger
der **Gegenstand, ⸚e** object, thing
das **Gegenteil, -e** opposite
die **Gegenwart*** presence
das **Geheimnis, -se** mystery, secret
die **Gelegenheit, -en** opportunity
das **Gelingen** success
das **Gemisch, -e** mixture
der **General, -e** or **⸚e** general
das **Geräusch, -e** sound
der **Geruch, ⸚e** smell
das **Geschick, -e** fate; skill
der **Geselle, -n** fellow
der **Gesichtspunkt, -e** point of view
die **Gesinnung, -en** feeling
die **Gewandtheit** skill
das **Glück*** luck; prosperity; happiness
der **Gott, ⸚er** god
der **(liebe) Gott** God
die **Große Los, -n -e** first prize (in lottery)
der **Grund*, ⸚e** reason
die **Gruppe, -n** group
die **Grüße** (mpl) wishes
das **Gute** good
die **Güte** kindness
die **Handlung, -en** action
die **Hauptsache, -n** the main thing
die **Herstellung, -en** manufacture
der **Hintergrund** background
das **Hin und Her** coming(s) and going(s)
die **Hoffnung, -en** hope
die **Höflichkeit, -en** politeness

die Höhe*, -n level
die Hygiene hygiene
die Idee, -n idea
die Instruktionen (fpl)
instructions
das Interesse, -n (an)
interest (in); interests
der Kampf*, ⁓e battle
das Kapitel chapter
die Katastrophe, -n
disaster
die Kenntnis, -se
information
der Kerl, -e fellow, chap
die Kerze, -n candle
die Kette*, -n series
der Kirchturm, -türme
steeple
der Klang, ⁓e sound
mit Klimaanlage air-
conditioned
der Klumpen lump
das Kommen und Gehen
coming(s) and going(s)
die Kondition, -en
condition
unter diesen Kondi-
tionen in these conditions
die Konstruktion, -en
construction
die Kontrolle, -n super-
vision
die Kopie, -n copy
der Korb*, -e basket
die Kosten expenses
der Kreis*, -e circle
der Krieg, -e war
der Kummer distress
das Lächeln smile
die Lage, -n situation

die Länge, -n length;
extent
die Lang(e)weile
annoyance; boredom
der Lärm noise
der Laut, -e sound
das Leben life
das Leid sorrow
der Leiter* chief; guide
die Leitung, -en super-
vision
der Leser, die Leserin
reader
das Licht, -er light
die Liebe, -n love
die Linie, -n line
die Liste, -n list
die Literatur literature
das Loch*, ⁓er opening;
hole
das Los, -e misfortune;
fate
die Lösung, -en solution
die Lücke, -n opening,
chink
die Lüge, -n lie
die Lust: ich habe Lust,
es zu tun I should love
to do it, I feel like doing
it
die Macht, ⁓e power
das Magazin, -e
magazine
der Mangel, ⁓ (an + dat)
lack (of), shortage (of)
die Mark* (Deutsch)-
mark
die Maschine, -n
machine
das Maximum, -a

maximum
die **Meinung, -en**
notice; opinion, view
meiner Meinung nach in
my opinion
das **meiste; die meisten**
most
die **Meldung, -en**
notice; announcement
die **Menge, -n** crowd
das **Minimum, -a**
minimum
die **Mischung, -en**
mixture
das **Mißgeschick, -e**
misfortune; disaster
das **Mitleid** sympathy
die **Mitteilung, -en**
message; communication
das **Mittel*** means
das **Modell, -e** version,
model
die **Möglichkeit*, -en**
means; possibility
sein Möglichstes tun to
do one's best
die **Moral** (sg) morals
die **Mühe** pains, trouble
die **Münze, -n** coin
der **Mut** courage, spirit
die **Nachrichten** (pl)
news; information
der **Nachteil, -e**
disadvantage
die **Nahrungsmittel**
(ntpl) provisions, food
der **Name*, -en**
reputation
die **Neigung, -en** slope;
inclination

das **Netz(werk), -e** and
(-e) network
das **Neue** (sg), die
Neuigkeit(en) news
das **Niveau, -s** level
die **Not** need, distress
die **Notiz, -en** notice
die **Nummer, -n** number
der **Nutzen** value
aus etwas Nutzen ziehen
to take advantage of
something
das **Objekt, -e** object
die **Öffentlichkeit**
public; publicity
die **Öffnung, -en** opening
die **Ordnung, -en** order
in Ordnung bringen to
arrange, tidy (up)
alles ist in Ordnung
everything is all right
der **Ort, -e** place
das **Pech, -e** misfortune,
bad luck
die **Pension*, -en** (old
age) pension
der **Pfeil, -e** arrow
das **Pfund, -e** pound
(sterling); pound (weight)
der **Plan, ⁼e** plan,
diagram
der **Platz*, ⁼e** place
die **Plauderei, -en** chat,
conversation
die **Politik** (sg) politics
das **Porträt, -s** portrait
das **Problem, -e** problem
das **Produkt, -e** product;
produce
die **Publizität** publicity

der **Punkt**, -e point
die **Qualität**, -en quality
der **Radau** hullaballoo
der **Rand**, ̈er edge, rim
der **Rat**, -schläge advice
das **Rätsel** mystery, puzzle
der **Rauch** smoke
der **Raum***, **Räume** space
Recht haben to be right
die **Rede**, -n speech
eine **Rede halten** to make a speech
die **Regierung**, -en government
die **Reihe***, -n series; line
ich bin an der Reihe it's my turn now
der **Reiz**, -e attraction, charm
die **Reklame**, -n advertisement
die **Reste** (*mpl*) remains, remnants
das **Resultat**, -e result
der **Revolutionär**, -e revolutionary
der **Rhythmus**, -men rhythm
die **Richtung**, -en direction
die **Rolle***, -n roll
die **Rückseite**, -n back (*of page etc*)
der **Ruf**, -e cry; reputation
die **Ruhe*** peace, calm
die **Sache**, -n thing; matter

die **Säule**, -n pillar
der **Schall**, -e sound, echo
der **Schein**, -e (bank)-note
ein 20 Mark Schein a 20-mark note
das **Schicksal** misfortune; fate
das **Schild**, -er sign
der **Schlag**, ̈e blow, bang, knock
die **Schließung** closure
der **Schluß**, ̈sse end(ing)
der **Schmutz**, die **Schmutzigkeit** dirt, dirtiness
der **Schnitt**, -e section
der **Schrei**, -e cry, scream
der **Schritt**, -e footstep; step, pace
die **Schüchternheit** shyness
die **Schuld** fault
ich bin nicht schuld daran it's not my fault
der **Schwatz**, ̈e chat, conversation
die **Schwierigkeit**, -en difficulty
die **Sensation** stir
die **Serie**, -n series
die **Sicherheit** security, safety
die **Sicht** sight; view
der **Sieg**, -e victory
der **Sinn**, -e mind; sense; meaning
die **Sitte**, -n custom

die **Situation**, -en
situation

die **Sorge**, -n care, worry
sich **Sorgen machen** to
be worried

die **Sorte**, -n sort, kind

das **Souvenir**, -s souvenir

der **Spalt** crack, opening,
split

die **Spalte**, -n column (of
page)

der **Spaß**, ̈e fun, joke

der **Spektakel** hullaballoo

das **Spielzeug**, -e toy

die **Spur**, -en sign, trace

der **Staat**, -en state

die **Staatskunst** (sg)
politics

der **Standpunkt**, -e point
of view

die **Stärke** power

das **Stelldichein**, -(s)
appointment

die **Stelle***, -n place

die **Steuer**, -n tax

der **Stil**, -e style

die **Stille** calmness

die **Stimmung**, -en
feeling

die **Strecke***, -n stretch,
distance

der **Strolch**, -e tramp

das **Stück***, -e piece, part

die **Summe**, -n sum

das **System**, -e system

das **Talent** talent

die **Tat**, -en act, action,
deed

in der Tat in (actual)
fact, indeed

die **Tätigkeit**, -en
activity

der **Teil**, -e, das **Teil**, -e
part, section

der **Text**, -e text

der **Titel** title

die **Tiefe**, -n depth;
thickness

der **Tor** fool

der **Traum**, ̈e dream

der **Treffpunkt**, -e
meeting place

der **Trost** comfort

die **Trümmer** (pl)
wreckage, ruins

der **Typ**, -en style;
version; chap

Überlebende(r), -n
survivor

das **Übermaß** excess

die **Überraschung**, -en
surprise

die **Umgebung**, -en
surrounding district

der **Umsturz**, ̈e
revolution

das **Unglück** disaster;
bad luck

das **Unheil** evil; disaster,
misfortune

unrecht haben to be
wrong, be mistaken

die **Unterbrechung**, -en
break, interruption

die **Unterhaltung**, -en
conversation, chat

die **Unternehmung**, -en
attempt; undertaking

der **Unterschied**, -e
difference

der **Urlaub, -e** holidays, leave

die **Ursache** reason, cause

die **Verabredung, -en** appointment

die **Verbannung** exile (*state*)

die **Verbindung, -en** connection

der **Vergleich, -e** comparison

das **Vergnügen** pleasure

das **Vermögen** wealth; power, ability

die **Version, -en** version

der **Versuch, "e** attempt, effort

das **Vertrauen** confidence

die **Vorbereitung, -en** preparation

der **Vorrat, die Vorräte** provisions

der **Vorschlag, "e** suggestion

die **Vorsicht** care

die **Vorstellung** introduction, idea; thought

der **Vorteil, -e** advantage

die **Wahl, "e** choice, selection; election

der **Wähler** elector

die **Wahrheit** truth

der **Wechselkurs, -e** exchange rate

die **Weile, -n** while

die **Weise, -n** way, method, manner

auf diese Weise in this way *or* manner

die **Weite** width

die **Werbung, -en** advertisement

der **Wert, -e** value

die **Wette, -n** bet

die **Wichtigkeit** importance

die **Wirklichkeit, -en** fact, reality

die **Wirkung, -en** effect

der **Witz, -e** joke

der **Wohlstand** prosperity

das **Wort, "er** word

die **Wünsche, -n** wish

die **Wut** anger, wrath

das **Zeichen** sign

die **Zahl, -en** number, figure

die **Zeile, -n** line (*of text*)

die **Zeitschrift, -en** magazine

die **Zeitung, -en** newspaper

das **Zentrum, Zentren** centre

das **Ziel** aim

das **Ziffer, -n** number, figure

der **Zorn** anger

das **Zutrauen** confidence

der **Zweck, -e** purpose

KONJUNKTIONEN UND PRÄPOSITIONEN

aber but; however

als when, as

also therefore, so

als ob, als wenn as if, as though

anstatt (+ gen) instead of

außer (+ dat) out of; except

außerhalb (+ gen) outside, outwith

bei (+ dat) near, by; at the house of

bevor before (time)

bis until, till (conj); (+ acc) until; (up) to, as far as

da as, since, seeing (that)

damit so that, in order that

denn for

ehe before

entweder . . . oder either . . . or

gegenüber (+ dat) opposite; to(wards)

gerade als just as

indem as, while

innerhalb (+ gen) in (side), within

je . . ., desto the more . . . the more

jemandem gegenüber opposite or towards somebody

nachdem after

nicht nur . . . sondern auch not only . . . but also

nun (da) now (that)

ob if, whether

obwohl although

oder or

ohne daß without

seit(dem) (ever) since

sobald as soon as

so daß; so . . . daß so that, so . . . that

so lange as long as

sondern (after neg) but

sowohl . . . als (auch) as well as, both . . . and

statt (+ gen) instead of

teils . . . teils partly . . . partly

trotz (+ gen) despite, in spite of

trotzdem, daß despite the fact that

und and

vorausgesetzt, daß provided that

während while (conj); (+ gen) during (prep)

weder . . . noch neither . . . nor

wegen (+ gen) because of

weil because

wenn when; if

wenn . . . auch although; even if

wie . . . auch however

VERBEN
abhängen von to depend on
jemanden abholen to fetch somebody, go and meet somebody
abreißen to demolish; to take down
(ab)schneiden to cut (up)
abschreiben to copy
abstürzen to crash
abwaschen to wipe
addieren to add
akzeptieren to accept
anbeten to adore
anbieten to give, offer
anblicken to look (at)
seine Meinung ändern to change one's mind
anfangen to begin
angeben to state
angehören (+ dat) to belong to (club etc)
angreifen to attack
anhalten to stop; to continue
ankleben to stick (on)
ankommen to arrive
ankündigen to announce
annehmen to accept; to assume
anschalten to switch on
anstarren to stare at
antworten to answer, reply
anzeigen to announce
anziehen to attract; to put (on) (clothes)
sich ärgern to get angry
aufbewahren to keep, store

aufgeben to abandon
aufhalten to block
aufhängen to hang (up)
aufheben to pick up
aufhören to stop, finish
aufkleben to stick on or onto
auflesen to pick, gather
aufmachen to open
aufpassen (auf + acc) to watch; to be careful (of), pay attention (to)
aufstellen to set up, fix (up)
auftreten to appear (on the scene)
aufwachen to wake up (intransitive)
aufwärmen to warm (up)
aufwecken to awaken, wake up (transitive)
ausdrücken to express
ausführen to carry out, execute
ausgeben to spend (money)
auslöschen to put out, extinguish
ausreichen to last
ausrufen to exclaim, cry (out)
sich ausruhen to rest
ausschalten to switch off
aussprechen to pronounce
ausstoßen to utter (cry)
ausstrecken to extend, hold out

sich ausstrecken to stretch out

auswählen to select

beabsichtigen to intend

sich (bei jemandem für etwas) bedanken to thank somebody for something

bedecken to cover

bedeuten to mean

bedienen to operate; to serve

sich beeilen to hurry

beenden to finish

befehlen (+ dat) to order

begegnen (+ dat) to meet

beginnen to begin

begreifen to realize

begründen to set up

behalten to keep, retain

behaupten to declare

beherrschen to rule (over)

sich beklagen (über + acc) to complain (about)

bekommen to obtain

beleuchten to light (up)

bemerken to notice

benachrichtigen to inform

beobachten to watch

berichten to report

(sich) beruhigen to calm down

sich beschäftigen mit to attend to; to be concerned with

beschmutzen to dirty

beschreiben to describe

(be)schützen (vor + dat) to protect (from)

besiegen to conquer

besitzen to possess, own

besorgen to provide

besprechen to discuss

bestehen (aus + dat) to consist (of), comprise

bestehen (auf + dat) to insist (upon)

bestellen to order

besuchen to attend, be present at, go to, visit

betätigen to operate

betreten to enter

beunruhigen to worry, disturb

(sich) bewegen to move

bewundern to admire

biegen to bend

bieten to offer

bilden to constitute, make up, form

binden to tie

bitten to request

bitten um to ask for

bleiben to stay, remain

blicken (auf + acc) to glance (at), look (at)

(sich dat) borgen to borrow; to lend

brauchen to need

brechen to break

brennen to burn

bringen to bring, take

sich bücken to stoop

danken (+ dat) to thank

darstellen to represent

dauern to last

decken to cover

denken to think, believe

denken an (+ acc) to

think of; to remember
denken über (+ *acc*) to think about; reflect on
deuten (**auf** + *acc*) to point (to *or* at)
dienen to serve
diskutieren to discuss
drehen to turn; to shoot (*film*)
drucken to print
drücken to press, squeeze
durchführen to accomplish, carry out
durchqueren to cross, pass through
durchsuchen to search (all over)
dürfen to be allowed to
eilen to rush, dash
einfallen (+ *dat*) to occur (*to someone*)
einladen to invite
einrichten to establish, set up
einschalten to switch on
einschlafen to fall asleep
einschlagen to break
eintreten to come in
eintreten in (+ *acc*) to come into, enter
einwickeln to wrap (up)
empfangen to receive (*person*)
empfehlen to recommend
entdecken to discover
entfalten to unfold
entführen to take away
enthalten to contain
entladen to unload
(sich) entscheiden to

decide
sich entschließen to make up one's mind
entschuldigen to excuse
sich entschuldigen (für) to apologize (for)
(sich) entwickeln to develop
sich ereignen to happen
erfahren to learn; to experience; **erfahren von** to hear about
ergreifen to seize
erhalten to receive, get
sich erheben to rise
erhellen to light (up)
sich erinnern (an + *acc*) to remember
erkennen to recognize
erklären to state; to explain
sich erkundigen (nach or **über** + *acc*) to inquire about
erlauben to allow, permit, let
erleben to experience
erleichtern to relieve
erleuchten to light
ermutigen to encourage
erobern to capture
erregen to disturb, excite
erreichen to reach; to accomplish
errichten to erect
erröten to blush
erschaffen to create
erscheinen to appear
erschrecken to frighten

erschüttern to shake, rock, stagger
erstaunen to astonish
erwachen to wake up
erwähnen to mention
erwarten to expect, await, wait for
erwidern to retort
erzählen to tell, explain
erziehen to bring up, educate
fallen to fall
fallen lassen to drop
falten to fold
fangen to catch
fassen to grasp; to comprehend
fehlen to be missing
etwas fertigmachen to bring something about; to get something ready
festbinden to tie
finden to find
fliehen (vor + *dat*, **aus)** to flee (from)
fließen (in + *acc*) to flow (into)
flüstern to whisper
folgen (+ *dat*) to follow
fordern to demand
fortgehen to go away
fortfahren to continue
fortsetzen to continue (*transitive*)
fragen to ask
sich fragen to wonder
sich freuen to be glad
führen to lead
füllen to fill
funkeln to sparkle

funktionieren to work (*of machine*)
sich fürchten (vor + *dat*) to be afraid *or* frightened (of)
geben to give
gebrauchen to use
gefallen (+ *dat*) to please; **das gefällt mir** I like that
gehorchen (+ *dat*) to obey
gehören (+ *dat*) to belong (to)
gelingen (+ *dat*) to succeed (in)
es gelang mir I succeeded
gelten to count; to be worth
genießen to enjoy
genügen to be sufficient
gernhaben to like
geschehen to happen
gewohnt sein zu to be(come) accustomed to
glauben (+ *dat*) to believe
glauben an (+ *acc*) to believe in
glühen to glow
sich etwas gönnen to indulge in something
gründen to establish
halten to keep; to stop; to hold
halten für to consider (as)
es handelt sich um it is a question of
hangen to be hanging
hängen to hang (up)

hassen to hate, loathe
hauen to cut, hew
heben to lift, raise
helfen (+ *dat*) to help
herangehen an (+ *acc*),
herantreten an (+ *acc*)
to approach
herausziehen to pull out
hereinkommen to enter,
come in
hereinlassen to admit
herstellen to produce,
manufacture
herumhantieren to
potter (about)
herumstreichen to stroll,
lounge about
herunterlassen to lower
hineingehen (in + *acc*)
to enter, go in (to)
hinlegen to put down
sich hinsetzen to sit down
hinstellen to put down
hinübergehen to go
through; to go over
hinuntergehen to go
down
hinweisen to point out
hinweisen auf (+ *acc*) to
refer to
hinzufügen to add
hoffen (auf + *acc*) to
hope (for)
holen to fetch
horchen to listen
hören to hear
hüten to guard, watch
over
interessieren to interest
sich für etwas interes-

sieren to be interested in
something
sich irren to be mistaken
kämpfen to fight
kennen to know (*person*,
place)
kennenlernen to meet,
get to know
klagen to complain
klatschen to gossip
klettern to climb
klingeln to ring
klingen to sound
knallen to crack; to
explode
knittern to crush
können to be able (to)
kriegen to get, obtain
sich kümmern (um) to
worry (about)
küssen to kiss
lassen to allow, let; to
leave
laufen to run
leben to live
legen to lay
sich legen to lie down
leid tun to grieve, hurt
es tut mir leid I'm sorry
sich (*dat*) **leihen von** to
borrow from
leiten to guide, lead
lesen to read
lieben to love
liegen to be (situated)
loben to praise
löschen to put out,
extinguish
lösen to buy (*ticket*)
losmachen to unfasten,

undo, untie
loswerden to get rid of
lügen to lie, tell a lie
malen to paint
meinen to think, believe
mieten to hire, rent
mitbringen to bring
mitnehmen to take
**jemandem etwas mit-
teilen** to inform some-
body of something
mögen to like
murmeln to murmur
müssen to have to (must),
be obliged to
nachdenken (über + acc)
to think (about)
nachsehen to check
nähen to sew
sich nähern (+ dat) to
approach
nähren to nourish; to
cherish
nehmen to take
sich neigen to lean
nennen to call, name
sich niederlegen to go to
bed, lie down
notieren to note
öffnen to open
organisieren to organize
passen (+ dat) to suit, be
suitable; be fit
passieren to happen
pflegen to take care of
ich pflegte zu tun I used
to do
plaudern to chat
pressen to press, squeeze
produzieren to produce

prüfen to examine
raten (+ dat) to advise
räumen to clear away
reiben to rub
reinigen to clean, tidy up
reisen to go, travel
rennen to run
retten to save, rescue
riechen (nach) to smell
(of)
rufen to call
sich rühren to stir
rühren (an + acc) to
touch
sagen (+ dat) to say (to),
tell
säubern to clean
saugen to suck
schaden (+ dat) to harm
schallen to sound
zu schätzen wissen to
appreciate
schauen (auf + acc) to
look (at)
scheinen to seem; to
shine
schieben to push, shove
schießen to shoot
schlafen to sleep
schlafen gehen to go to
bed
schlagen to hit, strike,
knock, beat
sich schlagen to fight
schleudern to hurl
(sich) schließen to close,
shut
schluchzen to sob
schmeicheln to flatter
schnappen to snatch

schneiden to cut
schnüren to tie
schreiben to write
schreien to shout, cry
schütteln to shake
schützen (vor + *dat*) to protect (from),
schwatzen to gossip
schweigen to be silent
schwören to swear
sehen to see
sein to be
senken to lower
setzen to put (down), place, set
sich setzen to settle, sit (down)
seufzen to sigh
sicherstellen to assure
singen to sing
sitzen to sit, be sitting
sollen ought (to)
sorgen für to take care of, look after
sich sorgen (um) to worry (about)
sparen to save
spaßen to joke
spazierengehen to go for a walk
stattfinden to take place
stehen to stand
stehenbleiben to stop (*still*)
steigen to come *or* go up, rise; to climb
stellen to put, place; to ask (*a question*)
sterben to die
stoppen to stop

(*transitive*)
stören to disturb
stoßen to push, shove
strecken to stretch
streiten to argue, fight
sich streiten to quarrel
stürzen to fall, crash
sich stürzen (in *or* auf + *acc*) to rush *or* dash (into)
suchen (nach) to look for, search for
tanzen to dance
teilen to share, divide
teilnehmen (an + *dat*) to attend, be present at, go to, take part (in)
töten to kill
tragen to carry; to wear
träumen to dream
treffen to meet; to strike
treiben to drive
trocknen to dry
tun to do
so tun, als ob to pretend (that)
überlegen to consider, reflect
überraschen to surprise
überreden to persuade
übertreffen to surpass
übertreiben to exaggerate
überwinden to overcome
(sich) umdrehen to turn round
umfassen to comprise
umgeben (von) to surround (with *or* by)
umgehen to avoid, bypass

umkehren to turn
umleiten to divert
umwerfen to overturn, knock over
unterbrechen to interrupt
unterhalten to support
(sich) unterhalten (über + acc) to converse or talk (about); to entertain
sich unterscheiden to differ, be different
unterschreiben to sign
untersuchen to examine
sich verabreden to make an appointment
verabscheuen to detest
verändern to change, alter
(sich) verbergen (vor + dat) to hide (from)
verbessern to improve
verbieten to forbid, prohibit
verbinden to connect
verbringen to pass or spend (time)
verdecken to hide, cover up
verderben to spoil, ruin
verdienen to deserve
vereinigen to unite
sich vereinigen to meet
vergessen to forget
sich verhalten to act, behave
verhindern to prevent
verhüten to prevent
verlangen to demand, order

verlängern to extend
verlassen to abandon
verleihen (an + acc) to lend (to)
verletzen to harm
verlieren to lose
es vermeiden, etwas zu tun to avoid doing something
vermieten to let, rent
versäumen to miss
(ver)schließen to lock
verschwinden to disappear, vanish
versehen (mit) to provide (with)
versichern (+ dat) to convince, assure
versprechen to promise
(sich) verstecken (vor + dat) to hide (from)
verstehen to understand
was verstehen Sie darunter? what do you understand by that?
versuchen to try, taste, sample; to attempt to
verteidigen to defend
verteilen to distribute
verursachen to cause, create
verzeihen to pardon, forgive
vollenden to finish
vorbereiten to prepare
vorgeben to pretend
vorhersehen to foresee
vorrücken to go forward
vorschlagen to suggest
(sich) vorstellen to

introduce (oneself)

sich etwas vorstellen to imagine something

wachen to watch

wachsen to grow

wagen to dare

wählen to elect; choose

warten (auf + *acc*) to wait (for)

(sich) waschen to wash

wechseln to exchange; to change (*money*)

wecken to awaken, wake up (*transitive*)

wegnehmen to take off *or* away

sich weigern to refuse

sich wenden an (+ *acc*) to apply to; to turn to

werden to become, grow, turn (out)

werfen to throw

wetten (auf + *acc*) to bet (on)

widmen (+ *dat*) to devote (to)

wiederholen to repeat

wiedersehen to see again

wischen to wipe

wissen to know

wohnen (in + *dat*) to live (in)

wohnen (**bei** + *dat*) to lodge (with), live (with)

wollen to want (to), wish (to)

sich wundern (über + *acc*) to wonder (at), be astonished (at *or* by)

es wundert mich I am surprised (at it)

das würde mich wundern! that would surprise me!

wünschen to wish

zählen to count

zeichnen to draw

zeigen to display, show

zerbrechen to break

zerdrücken to crush

zerreißen to tear

zerstören to demolish, destroy

zerstreuen to scatter

ziehen to draw; to pull; to tug

zittern (vor + *dat*) to tremble (with)

zögern to hesitate

zugeben to confess, admit

zugehen to close, shut (*intransitive*)

zuhören (+ *dat*) to listen (to)

zumachen to close, shut (*transitive*)

zurückkehren to come back, return

zurückkommen to go *or* come back

zurücksetzen, zurückstellen to replace

zusammenarbeiten to collaborate

zusammenstoßen to crash

sich zuwenden (+ *dat*) to turn towards

zweifeln to doubt

zwingen to force, oblige

HOMONYME
The following German words have more than one translation, depending on context. If you do not already know all these translations, check them up on the pages indicated, and then why not look for more?

das Alter 43, 122
der Anhänger 16, 32, 93
die Auskunft 31, 143, 147
das Bad 76, 119
der Balkon 78, 90, 176
das Band 86, 103
die Bank (pl ¨e) 56
die Bank (pl -en) 63, 147
der Berg 34, 108, 188
der Boden 18, 54, 76, 108
das Bowling 168
die Braut 43
der Bräutigam 42
das Brett 81, 192
die Brücke 31, 82, 173
die Chance 167, 218
die Dämmerung 195
die Decke 77, 82
das Eis 162, 194
die Entführung 150
die Fahrt 13, 31, 174
die Falte 103, 124
die Farbe 46, 65, 82
die Feder 153, 187, 193
die Fliege 49, 103
das Festland 190
der Flüchtling 149
der Flug 50
der Flügel 48, 52, 134, 186
die Frau 43, 123
die Führung 167
der Gang 12, 34, 76, 152
die Gang 147

die Garderobe 89, 178
die Gegenwart 206, 219
der Gepäckträger 30, 34
das Geschäft 25, 64, 174
der Geschäftsmann 26, 52, 65
die Geschichte 153
das Geschirr 21, 162
das Glas 114, 162, 198
das Gleis 31
die Größe 65, 123
der Grund 54, 219
die Hacke 56, 193
der Hahn 18, 83, 186
der Hausmeister 26, 76
die Höhe 52, 220
die Hütte 56, 79
das Kabel 191
der Kamin 76
der Kampf 166, 220
der Kanal 84, 189
die Karte 85, 176, 188
der Karton 114
die Kette 35, 92, 220
der Kiefer 107
die Kiefer 23
das Kissen 82
das Konzert 134
der Korb 34, 220
der Korridor 76
der Kreis 108, 220
die Kulissen 179
der Laden 62, 78, 172
das Land 19, 109, 188

INHALTSVERZEICHNIS

The vocabulary lists on the following pages contain the majority of nouns in the first two levels of the book, and will be a useful translation guide when you have a mental blank. A semi-colon between page numbers shows there will be a different translation depending on the context—simply look up the pages mentioned and the translation you require will be clear.